Scenes from Oscar Wilde

A collection of monologues and duologues for female actors

Compiled & edited by Kim Gilbert

Scenes from Oscar Wilde

Copyright © 2020 Kim Gilbert
All rights reserved.
ISBN: 9798649127431

Scenes from Oscar Wilde

DEDICATION

This collection of monologues and duologues for women taken from the plays and stories of Oscar Wilde is dedicated to all teachers and students of drama. I hope you gain as much satisfaction from his writing as I have.

ACKNOWLEDGEMENTS

A special thanks goes to my husband, Steve, who has prepared this book for publication. He has bailed me out on numerous occasions over the years with his technical expertise.

TABLE OF CONTENTS

Scenes from Oscar Wilde

Introduction	1
Biography	3
His Works	5
Writing Style	7
Playing Wilde	8
Famous Quotations	9
The Scenes	11
The Importance of Being Earnest	13
An Ideal Husband	33
The Canterville Ghost	55
A Woman of No Importance	57
Lady Windermere's Fan	71
Salome	83
The Nihilists	85
The Decay of Lying	87
The Duologues	89
The Importance of Being Earnest	91
A Woman of No Importance	101
Lady Windemere's Fan	104
About the Author	113

Scenes from Oscar Wilde

INTRODUCTION

I have compiled and edited this collection of monologues and duologues from the plays and writings of Oscar Wilde for young female actors to study as well as enjoy. These Classic scenes are suitable for a range of solo and duo acting exams as well as for auditions and festivals. This book is ideal for students and is a useful resource study for teachers of drama. I have tried and tested these scenes on numerous students over the years with great success and more importantly, they have thoroughly enjoyed working on them. It is crucial when choosing roles to perform to choose characters within ones' skill set and playing range.

The monologues and duologues in this collection are taken from a range of Oscar Wilde's plays: The Importance of Being Earnest, An Ideal Husband, Lady Windermere's Fan, A Woman of No Importance, Salome, The Nihilists and several of his short stories. There is a biography on Oscar Wilde, some notes about his writing style and a short synopsis of each play. Each scene has an introduction prepared suitable for exam or festival work and are also timed with exams and festival work in mind. I hope you enjoy this collection.

OSCAR WILDE

Oscar Fingal O'Flahertie Wills Wilde (1854-1900).

Oscar Wilde was born in Dublin, Ireland on October 16th 1854. He was the son of an ear and eye surgeon and a writer and poet mother, Jane Francesca Elgee. Wilde was greatly influenced by his mother and her linguistic abilities.

Oscar was originally baptised into the Church of Ireland (Anglican) and was later re-baptised into the Catholic faith. He was educated at home for the first nine years of his life until he went to Portora Royal school, Enniskillen, where he won the top prize for Classics. He was later educated at Trinity College, Dublin where he was awarded the Royal School Scholarship. He then went on to study at Magdalen College, Oxford. From Oxford, Wilde moved to London to pursue a literary career. Wilde's literary work was prolific and during his career moved to New York for nine months and delivered 140 lectures.

Oscar married Constance Lloyd in 1884. The couple had two sons together, Cyril and Vyvyan. The two boys were later to change their surnames from Wilde to Holland after their father's fall from grace. Constance moved to Switzerland with the two children in an attempt to avoid the scandal of her husband's notorious affair.

In 1891 he pursued an affair with Lord Alfred Douglas, whose nickname was Bosie. Unfortunately, this affair was rather public as Bosie was the son of the Marquis of Queensberry. Lord Queensberry was outraged by the public nature of this illegal relationship. In1895 Oscar Wilde sued Douglas's father, Marquis of Queensberry, for libel over accusations of homosexuality. Wilde lost the case and was arrested and imprisoned for 2 years. He was firstly incarcerated at Newgate prison, then at Pentonville prison and then transferred to Wandsworth prison, eventually ending his sentence in Reading Gaol. He was spat and jeered at on his transferral to Reading.The conditions were grim. At first, he was not even allowed writing materials but at a later date was granted these privileges. On release from prison, Wilde immediately went into exile to France. He never returned to

England. He died of meningitis in Paris aged 46yrs in 1900 and was buried there.

He was deeply committed to aestheticism throughout his life. Wilde received a posthumous pardon in 2017 when homosexuality was no longer considered a crime or illegal.

OSCAR WILDE'S WORKS

Writings, Novels, Plays, Essays, Poems

'Pall Mall Gazette'

First published collection, Poems (1881)

He edited Lady's World, a woman's magazine (1885)

The Duchess of Padua (1883)

Vera; or, The Nihilists (1880)

The Happy Prince and Other Tales (1888)

Lord Arthur Savile's Crime & other stories (1891)

Novel 'The Picture of Dorian Gray' (1891)

Plays

Lady Windermere's Fan (1892)

A Woman of No Importance (1893)

An Ideal Husband (1895)

The Importance of Being Earnest (1895)

Salome (1896)

Poetry

The ballad of reading Goal (1898)

Essays

The Decay of Lying: A dialogue

Pencil and Poison

The Soul of Man under Socialism

OSCAR WILDE'S WRITING STYLE

Oscar Wilde's writing style is unique. He writes with a mixture of realism and fantasy. His observation of character and social status puts him among the best of writers. His wit, intellect and use of satire is highly amusing, decadent and extremely critical. His plays are considered 'comedy of manners' and provide a satirical portrayal of behaviour amongst the upper echelons of Victorian society. His portrayal of wealth, snobbery and morality are insurmountable. He satirises the repression of the upper classes of Victorian Britain and examines the morality and philosophy of the period. His use of language is superb and his dialogue realistic. Oscar Wilde is by far one of the most influential writers of the nineteenth century.

AESTHETICISM

Oscar Wilde was a member of the aesthetic movement; a method used to promote or educate readers about important artistic expression in society. Aestheticism originated in France from Theophile Gautier. Oscar Wilde is considered the father of aesthetics in Britain. Other writers from this movement are: Algernon Charles Swinborne, Dante Gabriel Rossetti, William Morris, John Ruskin, Max Beerbohm and John Keats. The movement started during the 1860's by a group of artists, writers, and designers.They believed that literature should study beauty in its natural form. There should be an appreciation of the beauty of the writing or literature. Gautier (1811-1872) quoted "l'art pour l'art"; art for arts' sake. Writing should create a lasting, beautiful image and does not need to be political or didactic. It should be purely for the literary experience. It should be in the present, spontaneous, and in this respect, is considered hedonistic. In many ways, this style of writing emerged in retaliation from the oppression and puritanical aspect of Victorian society. Wilde certainly liked to cause a stir and pursued a hedonistic lifestyle. The movement believed good writing should affect the way we feel and should enhance our individual natural beauty. The reader should learn from the writing, whilst at the same time, appreciate the literary aspects of the writing: the use of grammar, rhythm, rhetoric and vocabulary. The components or aesthetic writing are: aesthetic fascination, aesthetic appraisal, aesthetic emotion and aesthetic perception.

Literature is crucial to our lives because it connects us to universal truths and ideas. Through literature, writers record their thoughts, feelings, experiences and share it with others through a fictional world.

Oscar Wilde considered that art was the only worthy element of life and the only thing worth living for. He lived his life in pursuit of beauty.

The association of Aestheticism also had an effect on costume and dress. There was a rejection of tightly laced corsets and a leaning towards natural fabrics. Oscar Wilde deplored Parisian couture, preferring natural, yet beautiful clothing. It is evident from his plays that he satirizes the manners and the restrictive, highly formalised costumes of the Victoria period.

PLAYING WILDE

It is essential to adopt the correct style of speaking when playing Wilde. Clipped, crisp diction and rounded vowel sounds are essential for this period. An awareness of the style of costume should also be considered. It is necessary to adopt the correct posture and elegance of the period. Knowledge of the use of the fan might be useful for playing some scenes.

QUOTES FROM OSCAR WILDE

- *"Life imitates art far more than art imitates Life".*

- *"Be yourself; everyone else is already taken"*

- *"I can resist everything except temptation".*

- *"I think that God, in creating man, somewhat overestimated his ability".*

- *"We are all in the gutter, but some of us are looking at the stars"*

- *"Some cause happiness where they go; others whenever they go".*

- *"Always forgive your enemies – nothing annoys them so much".*

- *"The books that the world calls immoral are books that show the world its own shame".*

- *"Education is an admirable thing, but it is well to remember from time to time that nothing that is worth knowing can be taught".*

- *"Experience is simply the name we give our mistakes".*

- *"One of the many lessons that one learns in prison is, that things are what they are and will be what they will be".*

- *"I always pass on good advice. It is the only thing to do with it. It is never of any use to oneself".*

- "What is a cynic? A man who knows the price of everything and the value of nothing".
- "I am not young enough to know everything".

THE SCENES

Scenes from Oscar Wilde

THE IMPORTANCE OF BEING EARNEST 1895

During Act One, two upper class bachelors, Algernon and Jack, are best friends and have fun pretending their names are Ernest, a popular man's name during the Victorian period. This enables them to lead double lives and this is where much of the comedy comes from. Jack Worthing likes to be known as Ernest in town, but Jack in the country. Algernon pretends to be named Ernest in order to woo Cecily Cardew as she is in love with the idea of marrying someone called Ernest. Both men are Bunburyists. A Bunburyist is the name given to someone who avoids their responsibilities by claiming to have to have appointments with non-existent individuals.It is a great excuse for getting out of family commitments.

Jack has a country home in Hertfordshire. He is the guardian of a pretty young 18yr old woman, named Cecily Cardew. She is the granddaughter of Jack's adopted father, Thomas Cardew. Cecily is being educated at home by a tutor, named Miss Prism. He concocts an alibi, claiming he has a brother named Ernest, who supposedly lives in London. In this way, he is able to escape to London to enjoy himself, away from the responsibilities he has on his estate.

Algernon has a cousin named Gwendolen Fairfax whom Jack has fallen in love with. He wishes to propose to her. Algernon confronts Jack over an inscription he finds in Jack's cigarette case from a woman named Cecily. Jack wishes to protect Cecily from men and is reticent for Algernon to meet her. This sparks an interest in discovering even more about Cecily and Algernon is eager to meet her. Jack confesses to Algernon that he is thinking of killing off his fake brother, Ernest, as Cecily is really keen to know more about him and things are becoming far too complicated.

Whilst Jack is visiting Algernon, Lady Bracknell arrives with her daughter, Gwendolen. Jack seizes the opportunity to propose to her. Gwendolen is also besotted by the name of Ernest and is determined to marry someone of that name. Jack has now created a dilemma for himself which is heightened by the fact that he is an orphan and is not seen at all eligible to marry Gwendolen.

During Act Two, whilst Jack remains in London, Algernon decides to pay a visit to Hertfordshire in order to meet Cecily. Cecily assumes Algy to be Jack's brother, Ernest. The two meet and are instantly attracted. Meanwhile, Jack decides to return from London with a story that his fake brother, Ernest, has unfortunately died in Paris. He is furious to find his story discredited due to the arrival of Algernon and immediately insists Algy should return to London. However, Cecily has fallen in love with her 'Ernest' and, due to her fascination with him, has already imagined that they have been engaged for the 'past three months'. The two men believe the only way to resolve their problem is to be christened in the name of Ernest. Both Jack and Algy separately arrange to be christened by Dr Chasuble. To make matters even more complicated, Gwendolen arrives to surprise Jack. She meets Cecily in the garden and the two share a rather frosty exchange as they assume, mistakenly, they are both in love and engaged with the same 'Ernest'. Matters are resolved when Gwendolen learns from Cecily that her Ernest is actually called Jack, and Gwendolen reveals to Cecily that her Ernest is in fact named Algernon. They confront the two bachelors together and are relatively appeased by the fact that both men tell them it was done for the love of the two women.

To complicate matters even further Lady Bracknell decides to follow her daughter, Gwendolen, to Hertfordshire and arrives shortly afterwards. She cross examines both couples as to their suitability as marriage partners but despite her reticence to Cecily, soon changes her mind when she discovers that Cecily is actually worth rather a lot of money. She still has a problem with Jack's lack of status and credentials. Jack manages to persuade her to change her mind with the revelation that as Cecily's guardian, he is not obliged to give permission for her to marry until she is 35 yrs of age. He will however agree to allow Cecily to marry Algernon on the proviso that he is in return able to marry Gwendolen. When Cecily's tutor Miss Prism, enters the scene, she panics. Lady Bracknell recognises Miss Prism as the governess who left her sister's house over twenty-eight years ago, over a scandal for losing a small baby. Miss Prism had mistakenly swapped the baby for a manuscript she had been writing and the baby had been left in a large handbag in a cloakroom at a train station. At this point, Jack has a revelation and realises that he is in fact this abandoned baby. He goes off in search of the handbag which he has kept for safe keeping, all these years. Jack is recognized as the long-lost baby of Lady Bracknell's sister. This makes Jack, Algernon's older brother. It also transpires that Jack was actually christened 'Ernest John'. The play ends happily with the two couples resolving their issues. Even Dr Chasuble and Miss Prism become a couple.

Scenes from Oscar Wilde

THE IMPORTANCE OF BEING EARNEST ACT 1

(Gwendolen and Lady Bracknell are visiting Algernon's house in London. Jack and Gwendolen are left alone for a moment and Gwendolen takes the opportunity to 'persuade' Jack that it is time for him to propose to her).

Gwendolen:
Pray don't talk to me about the weather, Mr Worthing. Whenever people talk to me about the weather, I always feel quite certain that they mean something else. And that makes me nervous. Yes, I am quite well aware of the fact that you have always admired me. And I often wish that in public, at any rate, you had been more demonstrative. For me you have always had an irresistible fascination. Even before I met you, I was far from indifferent to you. We live, as I hope you know, Mr Worthing, in an age of ideals. The fact is constantly mentioned in the more expensive monthly magazines, and has reached the provincial pulpits, I am told; and my ideal has always been to love some one of the name of Ernest. There is something in that name that inspires absolute confidence. The moment Algernon first mentioned to me that he had a friend called Ernest, I knew I was destined to love you.

My own Ernest!

But your name is Ernest. It suits you perfectly. It is a divine name. It has music of its own. It produces vibrations.

Jack? ... No, there is very little music in the name Jack, if any at all, indeed. It does not thrill. It produces absolutely no vibrations ... I have known several Jacks, and they all, without exception, were more than usually plain. Besides, Jack is a notorious domesticity for John! And I pity any woman who is married to a man called John. She would probably never be allowed to know the entrancing pleasure of a single moment's solitude. The only really safe name is Ernest.

Married, Mr Worthing?

I adore you. But you haven't proposed to me yet. Nothing has been said at all about marriage. The subject has not even been touched on. And to spare you any possible disappointment, Mr Worthing, I think it only fair to tell you quite frankly beforehand that I am fully determined to accept you.

Of course, I will marry you, darling. How long you have been about it! I am afraid you have had very little experience in how to propose...

Men often propose for practice. I know my brother Gerald does. All my girl-friends tell me so. What wonderfully blue eyes you have, Ernest! They are quite, quite blue. I hope you will always look at me just like that, especially when there are other people present.

THE IMPORTANCE OF BEING EARNEST ACT 1

(Jack has recently proposed to Gwendolen. Lady Bracknell has just discovered this proposal. She firstly addresses Gwendolen and then moves on to address Jack Worthing).

Lady Bracknell:
Mr Worthing! Rise, sir, from this semi-recumbent posture. It is most indecorous.

Pardon me, you are not engaged to anyone. When you do become engaged to someone, I, or your father, should his health permit him, will inform you of the fact. An engagement should come on a young girl as a surprise, pleasant or unpleasant, as the case may be. It is hardly a matter that she could be allowed to arrange for herself … And now I have a few questions to put to you, Mr Worthing. While I am making these inquiries, you, Gwendolen, will wait for me below in the carriage.

In the carriage, Gwendolen!

(Gwendolen leaves)

You can take a seat, Mr Worthing.

(She takes out a pencil and note book)

I feel bound to tell you that you are not down on my list of eligible young men, although I have the same list as the dear Duchess of Bolton has. We work together, in fact. However, I am quite ready to enter your name, should your answers be what a really affectionate mother requires. Do you smoke?

I am glad to hear it. A man should always have an occupation of some kind. There are far too many idle men in London as it is.

How old are you?

Twentynine? A very good age to be married at. I have always been of the opinion that a man who desires to get married should know either everything or nothing. Which do you know?

Nothing? I am pleased to hear it. I do not approve of anything that tampers with natural ignorance. Ignorance is like a delicate exotic fruit; touch it and the bloom is gone. The whole theory of modern education is radically unsound. Fortunately, in England, at any rate, education produces no effect whatsoever. If it did, it would prove a serious danger to the upper-classes and probably lead to acts of violence in Grosvenor Square. What is your income?

Between seven and eight thousand a year? In land, or in investments?

That is satisfactory. What between the duties expected of one during one's lifetime, and the duties exacted from one after one's death, land has ceased to be either a profit or a pleasure. It gives one position, and prevents one from keeping it up. That's all that can be said about land.

A country house! How many bedrooms? Well, that point can be cleared up afterwards. You have a town house, I hope? A girl with a simple, unspoiled nature, like Gwendolen, could hardly be expected to reside in the country.

A house in Belgrave Square. What number in Belgrave Square? 149. The unfashionable side. Are your parents living?

Lost both parents? To lose one parent, Mr Worthing, may be regarded as a misfortune; to lose both looks like carelessness.

Found!

Where did the charitable gentleman who had a first-class ticket for this seaside resort find you?

A hand-bag! In what locality did this Mr James or Thomas Cardew come across this ordinary hand-bag?

The cloak-room at Victoria Station?

The line is immaterial. Mr Worthing, I confess I feel somewhat bewildered by what you have just told me. To be born, or at any rate bred, in a hand-bag, whether it had handles or not, seems to me to display a contempt for the ordinary decencies of family life that reminds one of the worst excesses of the French Revolution. And I presume you know what that unfortunate movement led to? As for the locality in which the hand-bag was found, a cloak-room at a railway station might serve to conceal a social indiscretion – has probably, indeed, been used for that purpose before now – but it could hardly be regarded as an assured basis for a recognized position in good society. I would strongly advise you, Mr Worthing, to try and acquire some relations as soon as possible, and to make a definite effort to produce at any rate one parent, of either sex, before the season is quite over.

THE IMPORTANCE OF BEING EARNEST ACT 1

(Gwendolen wishes to speak privately to Jack so requests that Algernon should turn his back. Obviously, Algernon can hear every word expressed between the couple).

Gwendolen:
Algy, kindly turn your back. I have something very particular to say to Mr Worthing.

Ernest, we may never be married. From the expression on mamma's face I fear we never shall. Few parents nowadays pay any regard to what their children say to them. The old-fashioned respect for the young is fast dying out. Whatever influence I ever had over mama, I lost at the age of three. But although she may prevent us from becoming man and wife, and I may marry someone else, and marry often, nothing that she can possibly do can alter my eternal devotion to you.

The story of your romantic origin, as related to me by mamma, with unpleasing comments, has naturally stirred the deeper fibres of my nature. Your Christian name has an irresistible fascination. The simplicity of your character makes you exquisitely incomprehensible to me. Your town address at the Albany I have. What is your address in the country?

The Manor House, Woolton, Hertfordshire? There is a good postal service, I suppose? It may be necessary to do something desperate. That of course will require serious consideration. I will communicate with you daily.

Good! Algy, you may turn around now.

THE IMPORTANCE OF BEING EARNEST ACT 2

(Miss Prism is Cecily's governess and tutor. Cecily always seems to be a little distracted and Miss Prism is trying to encourage her to study).

Miss Prism:
Cecily, Cecily! Surely such a utilitarian occupation as the watering of flowers is rather Moulton's duty than yours? Especially at a moment when intellectual pleasures await you. Your German grammar is on the table. Pray open it at page fifteen. We will repeat yesterday's lesson.

Child, you know how anxious your guardian is that you should improve yourself in every way. He laid particular stress on your German, as he was leaving for town yesterday. Indeed, he always lays stress on your German when he is leaving for town.
Your guardian enjoys the best of health, and his gravity of demeanour is especially to be commended in one so comparatively young as he is. I know no one who has a higher sense of duty and responsibility. Mr Worthing has many troubles in his life. Idle merriment and triviality would be out of place in his conversation. You must remember his constant anxiety about that unfortunate young man his brother. I am not in favour of this modern mania for turning bad people into good people at a moment's notice. As a man sows, so let him reap. You must put away your diary, Cecily, I really don't see why you should keep a diary at all.

Memory, my dear Cecily, is the diary that we all carry about with us.

THE IMPORTANCE OF BEING EARNEST ACT 2

(Algernon has decided to visit Cecily in the country, knowing full well that Jack is safely in London).

Cecily:

(Merriman brings a silver salver with a calling card from Algernon on it).

Mr Ernest Worthing, B.4. The Albany'. Uncle Jack's brother! Did you tell him Mr Worthing was in town?

Ask Mr Ernest Worthing to come here. I suppose you had better talk to the housekeeper about a room for him.

(Algernon enters)

Mr Worthing. I am your cousin Cecily. You, I see from your card, are Uncle Jack's brother, my cousin Ernest, my wicked cousin Ernest.

I hope you have not been leading a double life, pretending to be wicked and being really good all the time. That would be hypocrisy. I can't understand how you are here at all. Uncle Jack won't be back till Monday afternoon. I think you had better wait till Uncle Jack arrives. I know he wants to speak to you about your emigrating. Your emigrating. He has gone up to buy your outfit. Uncle Jack is sending you to Australia.

Well, he said at dinner on Wednesday night, that you would have to choose between this world, the next world, and Australia.

Reform you? I'm afraid I've not time, this afternoon.
You are looking a little worse. That's because you are hungry. How thoughtless of me. I should have remembered that when one is going to lead an entirely new life, one requires regular and wholesome meals. Won't you come in?

THE IMPORTANCE OF BEING EARNEST ACT 2

(Cecily and Algernon are alone in the garden. Cecily, much to Algernon's astonishment, tells him they are already engaged and have been so for the past three months).

Cecily Cardew:
I don't think that you should tell me you love me wildly, passionately, devotedly, hopelessly. Hopelessly doesn't make much sense, does it?

Uncle Jack would be very much annoyed if he knew you were staying on till next week at the same hour.

You silly boy! Why, we have been engaged for the last three months. It will be exactly three months on Thursday.

Well, ever since dear Uncle Jack first confessed to us that he had a younger brother who was very wicked and bad, you, of course, have formed the chief topic of conversation between myself and Miss Prism. And of course, a man who is very much talked about is always very attractive. One feels there must be something in him after all. I daresay, it was foolish of me, but I fell in love with you, Ernest.

On the 14th of February last. Worn out by your entire ignorance of my existence, I determined to end the matter one way or the other, and after a long struggle with myself I accepted you under this dear old tree here. The next day, I brought this little ring in your name, and this bangle with a true lover's knot, which I promised you always to wear. You have wonderfully good taste, Ernest. It's the excuse I've always given you for leading such a bad life.

And this is the box in which I keep all your dear letters. I remember only too well that I was forced to write your letters for you. I always wrote three times a week and sometimes oftener. I couldn't possibly let you read them: they would make you far too conceited. The three you wrote me after we had broken off the engagement are so beautiful, and yet so badly spelled, that even now I can hardly read them without just crying a little.

Our engagement was broken off on the 22nd of March, you can see the entry if you like. "Today broke of engagement with Ernest. Feel it is better to do so. The weather still continues to be charming". It would hardly have been a really serious engagement if it hadn't been broken off at least once. But I forgave you before the week was out. You dear, romantic boy. I don't think that I could break it off now that I have actually met you. Besides, there is of course, the question of your name. You must not laugh at me, darling, but it had always been a girlish dream of mine to love someone whose name was Ernest. There is something in that name that seems to inspire absolute confidence. I pity any poor married woman whose husband is not called Ernest. But I don't like the name of Algernon. I might respect you, Ernest, I might admire your character, but I fear that I should not be able to give you my undivided attention.

THE IMPORTANCE OF BEING EARNEST ACT 3

(Miss Prism, Cecily's governess, has had a lifetime to wonder what happened to the lost baby in the handbag. She has tried to bury her thoughts in education. Now, at long last, all is revealed).

<u>Miss Prism:</u>
Lady Bracknell, I admit with shame that I do not know. I only wish I did. The plain facts of the case are these. On the morning of the day you mention, a day that is forever branded on my memory, I prepared, as usual, to take the baby out in its' perambulator. I had also with me a somewhat old, but capacious hand-bag in which I had intended to place the manuscript of a work of fiction that I had written during my few unoccupied hours. In a moment of mental abstraction, for which I never can forgive myself, I deposited the manuscript in the bassinette and placed the baby in the hand-bag.

Do not ask me, Mr Worthing.

I left it in the cloak-room of one of the larger railway stations in London.

The Brighton line.

(The hand-bag is exhibited)

It seems to be mine. Yes, here is the injury it received through the upsetting of a Gower Street omnibus in younger and happier days. Here is the stain on the lining caused by the explosion of a temperance beverage, an incident that occurred at Leamington. And here, on the lock, are my initials. I had forgotten that in an extravagant mood I had them placed there. The bag is undoubtedly mine. I am delighted to have it so unexpectedly restored to me. It has been a great inconvenience being without it all these years.

You?

Mr Worthing! I am unmarried!

Mr Worthing, there is some error.

(*Pointing to Lady Bracknell*).

There is the lady who can tell you who you really are.

THE IMPORTANCE OF BEING EARNEST ACT 3

(Lady Bracknell interrogates Miss Prism about the loss of the baby in the perambulator over twenty-eight years ago).

Lady Bracknell:
Miss Prism! Did I hear you mention a Miss Prism?

Pray allow me to detain you for a moment. This matter may prove to be one of vital importance to Lord Bracknell and myself. Is this Miss Prism a female of repellent aspect, remotely connected with education?

It is obviously the same person. I must see her at once. Let her be sent for.

(*Miss Prism enters*)

Prism! Come here, Prism! Prism! Where is that Baby?
Twenty-eight years ago, Prism, you left Lord Bracknell's house, Number 104, Upper Grosvenor Square, in charge of a perambulator that contained a baby of the male sex. You never returned. A few weeks later, through the elaborate investigations of the Metropolitan police, the perambulator was discovered at midnight standing by itself in a remote corner of Bayswater. It contained the manuscript of a three-volume novel of more than usually revolting sentimentality. But the baby was not there.

Prism! Where is that baby?

THE IMPORTANCE OF BEING EARNEST ACT 3

(Lady Bracknell is less than happy with Jack's proposal to Gwendolen).

Lady Bracknell:
Come here. Sit down. Sit down immediately. Hesitation of any kid is a sign of mental decay in the young, of physical weakness in the old. (*She turns to Jack*). Apprised, sir, of my daughter's sudden flight by her trusty maid, whose confidence I purchased by means of a small coin, I followed her at once by a luggage train. Her unhappy father is, I am glad to say, under the impression that she is attending a more than usually lengthy lecture by the University Extension Scheme on the Influence of a permanent income on Thought. I do not propose to undeceive him. Indeed, I have never undeceived him on any question. I would consider it wrong. But of course, you will clearly understand that all communication between yourself and my daughter must cease immediately from this moment. On this point, as indeed on all points, I am firm.

I do not know whether there is anything peculiarly exciting in the air of this particular part of Hertfordshire, but the number of engagements that go on seems to me considerably above the proper average that statistics have laid down for our guidance. I think some preliminary inquiry on my part would not be out of place. Mr Worthing, is Miss Cardew at all connected with any of the larger railway stations in London? I merely desire information. Until yesterday, I had no idea that there were any families or persons whose origin was a Terminus.

THE IMPORTANCE OF BEING EARNEST ACT 3

(Lady Bracknell agrees to allow Cecily to marry Algernon, now that she has discovered that Cecily is a wealthy young woman in her own right).

Lady Bracknell:
A moment, Mr Worthing. A hundred and thirty thousand pounds! And in the funds! Miss Cardew seems to me a most attractive young lady, now that I look at her. Few girls of the present day have any really solid qualities, any of the qualities that last, and improve with time. We live, I regret to say, in an age of surfaces. (*To Cecily*). Come over here, dear. Pretty child! Your dress is sadly simple, and your hair seems almost as Nature might have left it. But we can soon alter all that. A thoroughly experienced French maid produces a really marvelous result in a very brief space of time. I remember recommending one to young Lady Lancing, and after three months her own husband did not know her.

Kindly turn round, sweet child. No, the side view is what I want.

Yes, quite as I expected. There are distinct social possibilities in your profile. The two weak points in our age are its want of principle and its' want of profile. The chin a little higher, dear. Style largely depends on the way the chin is worn. They are worn very high, just at present, Algernon!

There are distinct social possibilities in Miss Cardew's profile. Never speak disrespectfully of Society, Algernon. Only people who can't get into it do that.

(*To Cecily*) Dear child, of course you know that Algernon has nothing but his debts to depend upon. But I do not approve of mercenary marriages. When I married Lord Bracknell I had no fortune of any kind. But I never dreamed for a moment of allowing that to stand in my way. Well, I suppose I must give my consent.

Cecily, you may kiss me!

You may also address me as Aunt August for the future. The marriage, I think, had better take place quite soon. To speak frankly, I am not in favour of long engagements. They give people the opportunity of finding out each other's character before marriage, which I think is never advisable.

Scenes from Oscar Wilde

AN IDEAL HUSBAND (1895)

Act One opens with an evening party hosted by Sir Robert Chiltern and his wife, Lady Gertrude Chiltern. Amongst the guests are Lord Goring, Mabel Chiltern (Sir Robert's sister) and an unannounced guest, Mrs Cheveley, who has attended the party with her friend, Lady Markby. Mrs Cheveley knows Lady Chiltern from her school days and is also acquainted with Lord Chiltern through a previous business scheme. She is eager to gain support from Sir Robert for an Argentinian Canal scheme and is willing to blackmail him in order to gain this support. Mrs Cheveley's mentor, Baron Arnheim, before his death, provided her with evidence from years ago, that Sir Robert divulged a cabinet secret regarding the Suez Canal. This scheme subsequently made them both wealthy. Sir Robert succumbs to the blackmail threat and endeavours to keep things quiet. However, on discovering her husband's agreement, Sir Robert is forced to change his mind by his extremely upright wife. Lady Chiltern is moralistically pure and refuses to allow her husband to have dealings with such an unscrupulous project. She is unaware of the blackmail threat. At the party, Lord Goring finds a diamond brooch and gives it, for safe keeping, to Mabel, until its' rightful owner is discovered.

In Act Two, Lord Goring, a trustworthy friend of Sir Robert's, implores him to divulge the truth about Mrs Cheveley's hold over him to Lady Chiltern. Lord Goring knows Mrs Cheveley only too well, having been previously engaged to her and knows she is untrustworthy. Lord Goring flirts with Mabel Chiltern. The two are very fond of each other and extremely well suited. He urges Sir Robert to reveal all to his wife and then goes on to try to persuade Lady Chiltern to be more flexible in her moralistic outlook. Mrs Cheveley arrives back at the house, in search of her lost brooch. She has also learned that Sir Robert has changed his mind about the scheme and is determined to reveal all to Lady Chiltern. Lady Chiltern is unforgiving of her husband when she discovers the details of his involvement with the Suez scheme.

In Act Three, the scene takes place at Lord Goring's home. He has received a letter, written on pink writing paper, from Lady Chiltern, begging him to help her resolve her problems. During the scene, Lord Caversham, Lord Goring's father, arrives stating it is high time his son considered marriage. Lord Chiltern also arrives to discuss matters with Lord Goring. Mrs Cheveley arrives unexpectedly. The butler shows her in, assuming she has an appointment, and whilst waiting for Lord Goring, discovers Lady Chiltern's letter on his desk. On learning that Mrs Cheveley is at the house, Sir Robert jumps to the wrong conclusion, assuming she and Lord Goring are having an affair. He walks out. Mrs Cheveley proposes to exchange the blackmail letter she has for Robert Chiltern for marriage to Lord Goring. She claims to still be in love with him. At this point, Lord Goring exhibits the diamond brooch to Mrs Cheveley. He reveals that he knows it is a stolen piece of jewellery. He insists that she give him the incriminating letter in exchange for not informing the police. She hands Goring the letter and he destroys it by burning it in the fire. However, on exiting, Mrs Cheveley steals Lady Chiltern's letter from Lord Goring's desk with the objective of suggesting it is a love letter from Gertrude Chiltern.

In Act Four, we discover that Sir Robert has denounced the controversial Argentinian Canal scheme. The matter of the letter is cleared up as Sir Robert believes it to be an apologetic love letter from his wife to himself. Lord Goring proposes to Mabel Chiltern but Sir Robert refuses her hand in marriage as he is convinced that Goring has been having an affair with Mrs Cheveley. Lady Chiltern then has to reveal the truth about the letter she has written. There is forgiveness all round and Sir Robert agrees to his sister, Mabel, marrying Lord Goring.

AN IDEAL HUSBAND ACT 1

(Mrs Cheveley is in discussion with Sir Robert Chiltern. They have not seen each other for a number of years. The scene takes place in Sir Robert Chiltern's house in Grosvenor Square, London. Mrs Cheveley has turned up to an evening party with her friend, Lady Markby, unexpectedly and uninvited. She attempts to blackmail Sir Robert).

Mrs Cheveley:

My stay in England really depends on you, Sir Robert.
I want to talk to you about a great political and financial scheme, about this Argentine Canal Company, in fact. You, I know, are interested in International Canal schemes. You were Lord Radley's secretary, weren't you, when the Government bought the Suez Canal shares?

I have invested very largely in the Argentine scheme. Baron Arnheim advised me. It was his last romance. His last but one, to do him justice.

I am not in a mood tonight for silver twilights, or rose-pink dawns. I want to talk business.

Sir Robert, I will be quite frank with you. I want you to withdraw the report that you had intended to lay before the House, on the grounds that you have reason to believe that the Commissioners have been prejudiced or misinformed, or something. Then I want you to say a few words to the effect that the Government is going to reconsider the question, and that you have reason to believe that the Canal, if completed, will be of great international value. You know the sort of things ministers say in cases of this kind. A few ordinary platitudes will do. In modern life nothing produces such an effect as a good platitude. It makes the whole world kin. Will you do that for me?
I am quite serious.

And if you do what I ask you, I ... will pay you very handsomely!

How very disappointing! And I have come all the way from Vienna in order that you should thoroughly understand me.

My dear Sir Robert, you are a man of the world, and you have your price, I suppose. Everybody has nowadays. The drawback is that more people are so dreadfully expensive. I know I am. I hope you will be more reasonable in your terms.

I realise that I am talking to a man who laid the foundation of his fortune by selling to a Stock Exchange speculator a Cabinet secret. I mean that I know the real origin of your wealth and your career, and I have got your letter, too.

The letter you wrote to Baron Arnheim, when you were Lord Radley's secretary, telling the Baron to buy Suez Canal shares – a letter written three days before the Government announced its own purchase. You thought the letter had been destroyed. How foolish of you! It is in my possession.

It was a swindle, Sir Robert. Let us call things by their proper names. It makes everything simpler. And now I am going to sell you that letter, and the price I ask for it is your public support of the Argentine scheme. You made your own fortune out of one canal. You must help me and my friends to make our fortunes out of another! This is the fame of life as we all have to play it, Sir Robert, soon or later!

AN IDEAL HUSBAND ACT 1

(Mrs Cheveley has returned to London from Vienna. She gatecrashes a party at Sir Robert Chiltern's residence. She is determined to blackmail Sir Robert over a past indiscretion).

Mrs Cheveley:
My dear Sir Robert, what then? You are ruined, that is all! Remember to what a point your Puritanism in England has brought you. In old days nobody pretended to be a bit better than his neighbours. In fact, to be a bit better than ones neighbour was considered excessively vulgar and middle-class. Nowadays, with our modern mania for morality, everyone has to pose as a paragon of purity, incorruptibility and all the other seven deadly virtues – and what is the result? You all go over like nine pins – one after the other. Not a year passes in England without somebody disappearing. Scandals used to lend charm, or at least interest, to a man – now they crush him. And yours is a very nasty scandal. You couldn't survive it. If it were known that as a young man secretary to a great and important minister, you sold a cabinet secret for a large sum of money, and that that was the origin of your wealth and career, you would be hounded out of public life, you would disappear completely. And after all, Sir Robert, why should your sacrifice your entire future rather than deal diplomatically with you enemy? For the moment I am your enemy. I admit it. And I am much stronger than you are. The big battalions are on my side. You have a splendid position, but it is your splendid position that makes you so vulnerable. You can't defend it! And I am in attack. Of course, I have not talked morality to you. You must admit in fairness that I have spared you that. Years ago you did a clever, unscrupulous thing; it turned out a great success. You owe to it your fortune and position. And now you have got to pay for it. Sooner or later we all have to pay for what we do. You have to pay now. Before I leave you tonight, you have got to promise me to suppress your report, and to speak in the House in favour of this scheme ... I will be in the Ladies' Gallery tomorrow night at half-past eleven. If by that time – and you will have had heaps of opportunity – you have made an announcement to the House in the terms I wish, I shall hand you back your letter with the prettiest thanks, and the best, or at least

the most suitable compliment I can think of. I intend to play quite fairly with you. After all, one should always play fairly ... when one has the winning cards...

AN IDEAL HUSBAND ACT 1

(Mrs Cheveley is talking to Lady Gertrude Chiltern).

Mrs Cheveley:
What a charming house you have, Lady Chiltern! I have spent a delightful evening. It has been so interesting getting to know your husband.

I wanted to interest him in this Argentine Canal scheme, of which I dare say you have heard. And I found him most susceptible – susceptible to reason, I mean. A rare thing in a man. I converted him in ten minutes. He is going to make a speech in the House to-morrow night in favour of the idea. We must go to the Ladies' Gallery and hear him! It will be a great occasion!

(Sir Robert & Lord Goring enter)

I don't regret my tedious journey from Vienna now. It has been a great success. But, of course, for the next twenty-four hours the whole thing is a dead secret. Between your husband and myself. Good-evening, Lady Chiltern! I am at Claridges.

Will you see me down, Sir Robert? Now that we have both the same interests at heart, we shall be great friends, I hope!

AN IDEAL HUSBAND ACT 1

(Lady Chiltern confronts her husband, Sir Robert, over his support of the Argentine Canal scheme. At this moment, she does not realise that Mrs Cheveley intends to blackmail him).

<u>Lady Chiltern:</u>
Robert, it is not true, is it? You are not going to lend your support to this Argentine speculation? You couldn't!

That woman who has just gone out, Mrs Cheveley, as she calls herself now. She told me. She seemed to taunt me with it. Robert, I know this woman. You don't. We were at school together. She was untruthful, dishonest, an evil influence on every one who trust or friendship she could win. I hated, I despised her. She stole things, she was a thief. She was sent away for being a thief. Why do you let her influence you? One's past is what one is. It is the only way by which people should be judged. It is a true saying, Robert. And what did she mean by boasting that she had got you to lend your support, your name, to a thing I have heard you describe as the most dishonest and fraudulent scheme there has ever been in political life?

But you told me yesterday that you had received the report from the Commission, and that it entirely condemned the whole thing. Robert! Oh! It is horrible that I should have to ask you such a question – Robert, are you telling me the whole truth?

It can never be necessary to do what is not honourable. Or if it be necessary, then what is it that I have loved? But it is not, Robert; tell me it is not. Why should it be? What gain would you get? Money? We have no need of that! And money that comes from a tainted source is a degradation. Power? But power is nothing in itself. It is power to do good that is fine – that, and that only. What is it, then? Robert, tell me why you are going to do this dishonourable thing!

Robert, that is all very well for other men, for men who treat life simply as a sordid speculation; but not for you, Robert, not for you. You are different. All your life you have stood apart from others.

You have never let the world soil you. To the world, as to myself, you have been an ideal always. Oh! Be that ideal still. That great inheritance throw not away – that tower of ivory do not destroy. Robert, men can love what is beneath them – things unworthy, stained, dishonoured. We women worship when we love; and when we have lost our worship, we havelost everything. Oh! Don't kill my love for you, don't kill that!

Scenes from Oscar Wilde

AN IDEAL HUSBAND ACT 1

(Lady Chiltern confronts her husband, Sir Robert, over his support of the Argentine Canal scheme. At this moment, she does not realise that Mrs Cheveley intends to blackmail him. She begs him to write a letter to Mrs Cheveley).

Lady Chiltern:
I know that there are men with horrible secrets in their lives – men who have done some shameful thing, and who in some critical moment have to pay for it, by doing some other act of shame - oh! Don't tell me you are such as they are! Robert; is there in your life any secret dishonor or disgrace? Tell me, tell me at once …It would be better for us both.

But why did you say those dreadful things, things so unlike your real self? Don't let us every talk about the subject again. You will write, won't you, to Mrs Cheveley, and tell her that you can't support this scandalous scheme of hers? If you have given her any promise you must take it back, that is all! You must never see her again, Robert. She is not a woman you should ever speak to. She is not worthy to talk to a man like you. No; you must write to her at once, now, this moment, and let your letter show her that your decision is quite irrevocable! She must know at once that she has been mistaken in you and that you are not a man to do anything base or underhand or dishonourable. Write here, Robert. Write that you decline to support this scheme of hers, as you hold it to be a dishonest scheme. Yes – write the word dishonest. She knows what that word means.

(Sir Robert sits down and writes a letter). Lady Chiltern reads it. Yes; that will do. *(She rings the bell).* And now the envelope. (T*o Mason, the butler)*

Have this letter sent at once to Claridge's Hotel.

Robert, love gives one an instinct to things. I feel to-night that I have saved you from something that might have been a danger to you, from something that might have made men honour you less than they do. I don't think you realise sufficiently, Robert, that you have brought into the political life of our time a nobler atmosphere, a finer attitude towards life, a freer air of purer aims and higher ideals – I know it, and for that I love you, Robert. I will love you always, because you will always be worthy of love.

AN IDEAL HUSBAND ACT 2

(Mabel Chiltern, is Sir Robert Chiltern sister. She is a lively young girl who is very popular. In this scene, she is visiting her sister in law, Gertrude. She is complaining of the fact that her brother's secretary, Tommy Trafford is paying her too much attention).

<u>Mabel Chiltern:</u>
Tommy Trafford is in great disgrace.

Gertrude, I wish you would speak to Tommy Trafford.

Well, Tommy has proposed to me again. Tommy really does nothing but propose to me. He proposed to me last night in the music-room, when I was quite unprotected, as there was an elaborate trio going on. I didn't dare to make the smallest repartee, I need hardly tell you. If I had, it would have stopped the music at once. Musical People are so absurdly unreasonable. They always want one to be perfectly dumb at the very moment when one is longing to be absolutely deaf. Then he proposed to me in broad daylight this morning, in front of that dreadful statue of Achilles. Really, the things that go on in front of that work of art are quite appalling. The police should interfere. At luncheon I saw by the glare in his eye that he was going to propose again, and I just managed to check him in time by assuring him that I was a bimetallist. Fortunately, I don't know what bimetallism means. And I don't believe anybody else does either. But the observation crushed Tommy for ten minutes. He looked quite shocked. And then Tommy is so annoying in the way he proposes. If he proposed at the top of his voice I would not mind so much. That might produce some effect on the public. But he does it in a horrid, confidential way. When Tommy wants to be romantic he talks to one just like a doctor. I am very fond of Tommy, but his methods of proposing are quite out of date. I wish, Gertrude, you would speak to him, and tell him that once a week is quite often enough to propose to anyone, and that it should always be done in a manner that attracts some attention.

I know, dear. You married a man with a future, didn't you? But then, Robert was a genius, and you have a noble, self-sacrificing character. You can stand geniuses. I have no character at all, and Robert is the only genius I could ever bear. As a rule, I think they are quite impossible. Geniuses talk so much don't they? Such a bad habit! And they are always thinking about themselves when I want them to be thinking about me. I must go around now and rehearse at Lady Basildon's. You remember we are having tableau, don't you? The Triumph of something, I don't know what! I hope it will be the triumph of me. Only triumph I am really interested in at present.

Oh, Gertrude, do you know who is coming to see you? That dreadful Mrs Cheveley in a most lovely gown! I assure you she is coming upstairs, as large as life and not nearly so natural.

AN IDEAL HUSBAND ACT 2

(Lady Markby and Mrs Cheveley are visiting Lady Chiltern, at home. They have come to ask if the brooch has been found).

Lady Markby:

Well, I must say it is most annoying to lose anything. I remember once at Bath, years ago, losing in the Pump Room an exceedingly handsome cameo bracelet that Sir John had given me. I don't think he has ever given me anything since, I am sorry to say. He has sadly degenerated. Really, this horrid House of Commons quite ruins our husbands for us. I think the Lower House by far the greatest blow to a happy married life that there has been since that terrible thing called the Higher Education of Women was invented.

I don't think man has much capacity for development. He has got as far as he can, and that is not far, is it? With regard to women, well, dear Gertrude, you belong to the younger generation, and I am sure it is all right if you approve of it. In my time, of course, we were taught not to understand anything. That was the old system, and wonderfully interesting it was. I assure you that the amount of things I and my poor dear sister were taught not to understand was quite extraordinary. But modern women understand everything, I am told.

But not their husbands? And a very good thing too, dear, I dare say. It might break up many a happy home if they did. Not yours, I need hardly say, Gertrude. You have married a pattern husband. I wish I could say as much for myself. But since Sir John has taken to attending the debates regularly, which he never used to do in the good old days, his language has become quite impossible. He always seems to think that he is addressing the House, and consequently whenever he discusses the state of the agricultural labourer, or the Welsh Church, or something quite improper of that kind, I am obliged to send all the servants out of the room. It is not pleasant to see one's own butler, who has been with one for twenty-three years, actually blushing at the sideboard, and the footmen making contortions in corners like persons in circuses. I assure you my life will be quite ruined unless they send John at once to the Upper House. He won't take any interest in politics then, will he? The House of Lords is so sensible. An assembly of gentlemen. But in his present state, Sir john is really a great trial. Why, this morning before breakfast was half over, he stood up on the hearth-rug, put his hands in his pockets, and appealed to the country at the top of his voice. I left the table as soon as I had my second cup of tea, I need hardly say. But his violent language could be heard all over the house! I trust, Gertrude, that Sir Robert is not like that?

AN IDEAL HUSBAND ACT 2

(Lady Markby, Mrs Cheveley and Lady Chiltern are having tea at the Chiltern household).

Lady Markby:
No tea, thanks, dear. The fact is, I have promised to go around for ten minutes to see poor Lady Brancaster, who is in very great trouble. Her daughter, quite a well-brought-up girl, too, has actually become engaged to be married to a curate in Shropshire. It is very sad, very sad indeed. I can't understand this modern mania for curates. In my time we girls saw them, of course, running about the place like rabbits. But we never took any notice of them, I need hardly say. But I am told that nowadays country society is quite honeycombed with them. I think it most irreligious. And then the eldest son has quarreled with his father, and it is said that when they meet at the club Lord Brancaster always hides himself behind the money article in *The Times*. However, I have to take in extra copies of *The Times* at all the clubs in St. James's Street; there are so many sons who won't have anything to do with their fathers, and so many fathers who won't speak to their sons. I think, myself, it is very much to be regretted.

You know Lady Brancaster, don't you, dear?

Well, like all stout women, she looks the very picture of happiness, as no doubt you noticed. But there are many tragedies in her family, besides this affair of the curate. Her own sister, Mrs Jekyll, had a most unhappy life; through no fault of her own, I am sorry to say. She ultimately was so broken-hearted that she went into a convent, or on to the operatic stage, I forget which. No; I think it was decorative art-needlework she took up. I know she had lost all sense of pleasure in life. *(rising).* And now, Gertrude, if you will allow me, I shall leave Mrs Cheveley in your charge and call back for her in a quarter of an hour. Or perhaps, dear Mrs Cheveley, you wouldn't mind waiting in the carriage while I am with Lady Brancaster. As I intend it to be a visit of condolence, I shan't stay long.

Ah yes! no doubt you both have many pleasant reminiscences of your schooldays to talk over together. Good-bye, dear Gertrude! Shall I see you at Lady Bonar's tonight? She has discovered a wonderful new genius. He does ... nothing at all, I believe. That is a great comfort, is it not?

Dining at home by yourselves? Is that quite prudent? Ah, I forgot, your husband is an exception. Mine is the general rule, and nothing ages a woman so rapidly as having married the general rule.

AN IDEAL HUSBAND ACT 3

(Mrs Cheveley is showed into Lord Goring's house by the footman. Whilst she is waiting, she discovers a letter written on pink paper on Lord Goring's desk).

Mrs Cheveley:
Lord Goring expects me?

Ugh! How dreary a bachelor's drawing-room always looks! I shall have to alter this. No, I don't care for that lamp. It is far too glaring. Light some candles.

I wonder what woman he is waiting for to-night. It will be delightful to catch him. Men always look so silly when they are caught. And they are always being caught. What a very interesting room! What a very interesting picture! Wonder what his correspondence is like.

(She looks through his letter on the writing-table).

Oh, what a very uninteresting correspondence! Bills and cards, debts and dowagers! Who on earth writes to him on pink paper? How silly to write on pink paper! It looks like the beginning of a middle-class romance. Romance should never begin with sentiment. It should begin with science and end with a settlement.

(She puts down the letter, then takes it up again).

I know that handwriting. That is Gertrude Chiltern's. I remember it perfectly. The ten commandments in every stroke of the pen, and the moral law all over the page. Wonder what Gertrude is writing to him about? Something horrid about me, I suppose. How I detest that woman!

(She reads the letter).

'I trust you. I want you. I am coming to you. Gertrude.' 'I trust you. I want you. I am coming to you'.

(She is just about to steal the letter when Phipps, the butler

enters. She slips the letter under a large silver-cased blotting book that is lying on the table).

Scenes from Oscar Wilde

AN IDEAL HUSBAND ACT 3

(Mrs Cheveley is talking to Lord Goring. She tells him she will withdraw her blackmailing plot in return for marriage with him. She also confesses she hates Gertrude Chiltern).

Mrs Cheveley:
I don't mind bad husbands. I have had two. They amused me immensely.

My dear Arthur, women are never disarmed by compliments. Men always are. That is the difference between the two sexes. You are going to allow your greatest friend, Robert Chiltern, to be ruined, rather than marry someone who really has considerable attractions left. I thought you would have risen to some great height of self-sacrifice, Arthur. I think you should. And the rest of your life you could spend in contemplating your own perfections. As if anything could demoralize Robert Chiltern! You seem to forget that I know his real character. How you men stand up for each other! I only war against one woman, against Gertrude Chiltern. I hate her. I hate her now more than ever. Oh, there is only one real tragedy in a woman's life. The fact that her past is always her lover, and her future invariably her husband.

A woman whose size in gloves is seven and three quarters never knows much about anything. You know Gertrude has always worn seven and three quarters? That is one of the reasons why there was never any moral sympathy between us ... Well, Arthur, I suppose this romantic interview may be regarded as at an end. You admit it was romantic, don't you? For the privilege of being your wife I was ready to surrender a great prize, the climax of my diplomatic career. You decline. Very well, If Sir Robert doesn't uphold my Argentine scheme, I expose him. *Voila tout.*

Oh, don't use big words. They mean so little. It is a commercial transaction. That is all. There is no good mixing up sentimentality in it. I offered to sell Robert Chiltern a certain thing. If he won't pay me my price, he will have to pay the world a greater price. There is no more to be said. I must go. Good-bye. Won't you shake hands?

Arthur, you are unjust to me. Believe me, you are quite unjust to me. I didn't go to taunt Gertrude at all. I had no idea of doing anything of the kind when I entered. I called with Lady Markby simply to ask whether an ornament, a jewel, that I lost somewhere last night, had been found at the Chilterns. If you don't believe me, you can ask Lady Markby. She will tell you it is true. The scene that occurred happened after Lady Markby had left, and was really forced on me by Gertrude's rudeness and sneers. I called – a little out of malice if you like – but really to ask if a diamond brooch of mine had been found.

THE CANTERVILLE GHOST (1887)

(This is a short story about a young girl who befriends a ghost which is haunting Canterville Chase. The young girls assists him in moving on into the afterlife. The ghost is haunting the castle as he murdered his wife there. Virginia Otis is 15yr old young girl who is talking to the Canterville ghost, Sir Simon de Canterville. The Otis's are an American family who have purchased Canterville Chase. Virginia sympathises with the ghost).

Virginia:
I am so sorry for you, but my brothers are going back to Eton tomorrow, and then, if you behave yourself, no one will annoy you. It is no reason at all for existing, and you know you have been very wicked. Mrs Umney told us, the first day we arrived here, that you had killed your wife.

It is very wrong to kill anyone. Starved you to death? Oh, Mr Ghost, I mean Sir Simon, are you hungry? I have a sandwich in my case. Would you like it?

Stop! It is you who are rude and horrid, and vulgar and, as for dishonesty, you know you stole the paints out of my box t try and furbish up that ridiculous blood stain in the library. First you took all my reds, including the vermilion, and I couldn't do any more sunsets, then you took the emerald green and the chrome yellow, and finally I had nothing left but indigo and Chinese white, and could only do moonlight scenes which are always depressing to look at, and not at all easy to paint. I never told on you, though I was very much annoyed, and it was most ridiculous, the whole thing; for who ever heard of emerald green blood? The best thing you can do is to emigrate and improve your mind. My father will be only too happy to give you a free passage, and though there is a heavy duty on spirits of every kind, there will be no difficulty about the Custom House, as the officers are all Democrats. Once in New York you are sure to be a great success. I know lots of people there who would give a hundred thousand dollars to have a grandfather, and much more than that to have a family ghost … one who has been … and you know you have been … very wicked.

Not like America? I suppose because we have no ruins and no curiosities.

You haven't slept for three hundred years? That's quite absurd! You have merely to go to bed and blow out the candle. It is very difficult sometimes to keep awake, especially at church, but there is no difficulty at all about sleeping. Why, even babies know how to do that, and they are not very clever.

Poor, poor Ghost. Have you no place where you can sleep?

You mean the Garden of Death.

I am not afraid of you and I will ask the Angel to have mercy on you.

A WOMAN OF NO IMPORTANCE (1893)

Act One takes place at Lady Hunstanton's estate. Her guests are Lady Caroline Pontefract, Mrs Allonby Lady Stuttfield and Hester Worsley, a young, wealthy and opinionated American woman who is visiting Britain for the first time. Gerald Arbuthnot has been appointed secretary to Lord Illingworth. To celebrate this promotion, his mother, Mrs Arbuthnot has been invited to the estate. Lord Illingworth is a flirtatious, political and ambitious figure. He has already expressed an interest in the young Hester Worsley and flirts openly with Mrs Allonby. Lord Illingworth spots a hand written letter from Mrs Arbuthnot on a table and recognises her handwriting.

In Act Two, Mrs Arbuthnot arrives. Her son Gerald introduces his mother to his new employer, Lord Illingworth, and there is an awkward atmosphere between the two. Lady Hunstanton asks her guests to withdraw to the music room and Lord Illingworth requests Mrs Arbuthnot stay behind to discuss matters of importance. It transpires that Gerald is the illegitimate son of Lord Illingworth who, on discovering the pregnancy many years ago, refused to marry Mrs Arbuthnot, despite offering to finance her secretly via his wealthy mother. Mrs Arbuthnot does not wish her son, Gerald, to work for Lord Illingworth, stating that after a miserable existence of shame and poverty, he is all she has in the world. Lord Illingworth tells her she should not jeopardise her sons' future.

In Act Three, Lord Illingworth lectures Gerald on society and marriage. He reveals he himself has never been married. Lord Illingworth agrees that his mother is a great woman but insists that Gerald should decide his own future. Gerald is becoming increasingly attracted to Hester Worsley. Gerald still does not yet know who his father is. After some entertaining discussions and arguments amongst the house guests, Mrs Arbuthnot decides to reveal the truth about Gerald's father. Gerald announces that he will be travelling to India with Lord Illingworth. Shortly afterwards, Hester enters complaining that Lord Illingworth has tried to kiss her. George is furious and Mrs Arbuthnot asks Gerald to take her home.

Act Four takes place at the home of Mrs Arbuthnot. Gerald writes a letter to Lord Illingworth asking him to marry his mother. He no longer wishes to be his secretary and insists that his father comes to the house by 4pm that day. Mrs Arbuthnot refuses to marry Lord Illingworth and on overhearing the argument between mother and son, Hester Worsley intervenes and insists that she will financially take care of Gerald, whom she loves, along with his mother. Mrs Arbuthnot will be treated like the mother she has never had. Lord Illingworth arrives and forces his way past the servants. He then reads Gerald's letter and agrees to marry Mrs Arbuthnot, for the sake of their son but Mrs Arbuthnot again rejects the proposal. Lord Illingworth learns that Gerald is to marry Hester and does not need his money. Lord Illingworth disgraces himself by suggesting his affair was trifling and Mrs Arbuthnot was merely his mistress. Mrs Arbuthnot's slaps him. Hester and Gerald return from the garden and realise that Lord Illingworth has visited. When they find his glove on the floor, Mrs Arbuthnot claims it belongs to "a man of no importance".

A WOMAN OF NO IMPORTANCE ACT 2

(In the drawing room at Hunstanton Chase. Mrs Allonby offers her views on the Ideal man. Lady Stutfield, Lady Hunstanton and Lady Caroline are with her).

Mrs Allonby:
Do you know, Lady Caroline, I don't think the frivolity of the wife has ever anything to do with it. More marriages are ruined nowadays by the common sense of the husband than by anything else. How can a woman be expected to be happy with a man who insists on treating her as if she was a perfectly rational being? Man, poor, awkward, reliable, necessary man belongs to a sex that has been rational for millions and millions of years. He can't help himself. It is in his race. The History of Woman is very different. We have always been picturesque protests against the mere existence of common sense. We saw it's dangers from the first.

The Ideal Husband? There couldn't be such a thing. The institution is wrong.

The Ideal Man! Oh, the ideal Man should talk to us as if we were goddesses, and treat us as if we were children. He should refuse all our serious requests, and gratify every one of our whims. He should encourage us to have caprices, and forbid us to have missions. He should always say much more than he means, and always mean much more than he says.

He should never run down other pretty women. That would show he had not taste, or make one suspect that he had too much. No; he should be nice about them all, but say that, somehow, they don't attract him.

If we ask him a question about anything, he should give us an answer all about ourselves. He should invariably praise us for whatever qualities he knows we haven't got. But he should be pitiless, in reproaching us for the virtues that we have never dreamed of possessing. He should never believe that we know the use of useful things. That would be unforgivable. But he should shower on us everything we don't want.

He should persistently compromise us in public, and treat us with absolute respect when we are alone. And yet he should be always ready to have a perfectly terrible scene, whenever we want one, and to become miserable, absolutely miserable, at a moment's notice, and to overwhelm us with just reproaches in less than twenty minutes and to be positively violent at the end of half an hour, and to leave us forever at a quarter to eight, when we have to go and dress for dinner. And when, after that, one has seen him for really the last time, and he has refused to take back the little things he has given one, and promised never to communicate with one again, or to write one any foolish letters, he should be perfectly broken-hearted, and telegraph to one all day long, and send one little notes every half hour by a private hansom, and dine quite alone at the club, so that everyone should know how unhappy he was. And after a whole dreadful week, during which one has gone about everywhere with one's husband, just to show how absolutely lonely one was, he may be given a third last parting, in the evening, and then, if his conduct has been quite irreproachable, and one has behaved really badly to him, he should be allowed to admit that he has been entirely in the wrong, and when he has admitted that, it becomes a woman's duty to forgive, and one can do it all over again from the beginning, with variations.

A WOMAN OF NO IMPORTANCE ACT 2

(Hester Worsley, an American heiress is visiting England. She expresses her views on the English aristocracy).

Hester:
I have been listening to the conversation. I didn't believe any of it. I couldn't believe that any women could really hold such views of life as I have heard tonight from some of your guests.

There are cliques in America, as elsewhere, Lady Hunstanton. But true American society consists simply of all good women and good men we have in our country. In America we have no lower classes.

The English aristocracy supply us with our curiosities, Lady Caroline. They are sent over to us every summer, regularly, in the steamers, and propose to us the day after they land. As for ruins, we are trying to build up something that will last longer than brick or stone.

We are trying to build up life, Lady Hunstanton, on a better, truer, purer basis than life rests on here. This sounds strange to you all, no doubt. How could it sound other than strange? You rich people in England, you don't know how you are living. How could you know? You shut out from your society the gentle and the good. You laugh at the simple and the pure. Living, as you all do, on others and by them you sneer at self-sacrifice, and if you throw bread to the poor, it is merely to keep them quiet for a season. With all your pomp and wealth and art you don't know how to live – you don't even know that. You love the beauty that you can see and touch and handle, the beauty that you can destroy, and do destroy, but of the unseen beauty of life, of the unseen beauty of a higher life, you know nothing. You have lost life's secret. Oh, your English society seems to me shallow, selfish, foolish. It has blinded its' eyes, and stopped its' ears. It lies like a leper in purple. It sits like a dead thing smeared with gold. It is all wrong, all wrong.

Lord Weston! I remember him, Lady Hunstanton. A man with a

hideous smile and a hideous past. He is asked everywhere. No dinner party is complete without him. What of those whose ruin is due to him? They are outcasts. They are nameless. If you met them in the street you would turn your head away. I don't complain of their punishment. Let all women who have sinned be punished. It is right that they should be punished, but don't let them be the only ones to suffer. If a man and woman have sinned, let them both go forth into the desert to love or loathe each other there. Let them both be branded. Set a mark, if you wish, on each, but don't punish the one and let the other go free. Don't have one law for men and another for women. You are unjust to women in England. And till you count what is a shame in a woman to be an infamy in a man, you will always be unjust, and Right, that pillar of fire, and Wrong, that pillar of cloud, will be made dim to your eyes, or be not seen at all, or if seen, not regarded.

I am afraid you think I spoke too strongly, Lady Hunstanton.

A WOMAN OF NO IMPORTANCE ACT 2

(Mrs Arbuthnot begs Lord Illingworth not to take her son, George, from her. He is all she has).

Mrs Arbuthnot:
You have no right to claim him, or the smallest part of him. The boy is entirely mine, and shall remain mine.

Are you talking of the child you abandoned? Of the child who, as far as you are concerned might have died of hunger and want?

I left you because you refused to give the child a name. Before my son was born, I implored you to marry me.

When a man is old enough to do wrong, he should be old enough to do right also.

I wouldn't have accepted a penny from your mother. Your father was different. He told you, in my presence, when we were in Paris, that it was your duty to marry me.

Gerald shall certainly not go away with you. Do you think I would allow my son – My son – to go away with the man who spoiled my youth, who ruined my life, who has tainted every moment of my days? You don't realise what my past has been in suffering and in shame.

Gerald cannot separate his future from my past. He was not discontented till he met you. You have made him so. I will not allow him to go. I have brought him up to be a good man.

George, don't take my son away from me. I have had twenty years of sorrow, and I have only had one thing to love me, only one thing to love. You have had a life of joy, and pleasure, and success. You have been quite happy, you have never thought of us. There was no reason, according to your views of life, why you should have remembered us at all. Your meeting us was a mere accident, a horrible accident. Forget it. Don't come now, and rob me of – of all I have in the whole world. You are so right in other things. Leave me the little vineyard of my life; leave me the walled-in garden, and the well of water; the ewe-lamb god sent me, in pity of in wrath, oh! Leave me that. George, don't take Gerald from me.

A WOMAN OF NO IMPORTANCE ACT 3

(Mrs Arbuthnot reveals to Gerald, the true nature of Lord Illingworth. Gerald will soon discover that Lord Illingworth is his father).

<u>Mrs Arbuthnot:</u>
Gerald, come near to me. Quite close to me, as you used to do when you were a little boy, when you were mother's own boy.

(Gerald sits beside his mother. She runs her fingers through his hair, and strokes his hands)

Gerald, there was a girl once, she was very young, she was a little over eighteen at the time. George Harford – that was lord Illingworth's name then – George Harford met her. She knew nothing about life. He – knew everything. He made this girl love him. He made her love him so much that she left her father's house with him one morning. She loved him so much, and he had promised to marry her! He had solemnly promised to marry her, and she had believed him. She was very young, and – and ignorant of what life really is. But he put the marriage off from week to week, and month to month. She trusted in him all the while. She loved him. – Before her child was born – for she had a child – she implored him for the child's sake to marry her, that the child might have a name, that her sin might not be visited on the child, who was innocent. He refused. After the child was born, she left him, taking the child away, and her life was ruined, and her soul ruined, and all that was sweet, and good, and pure in her ruined also. She suffered terribly – she suffers now. She will always suffer. For her there is no joy, no peace, no atonement. She is a woman who drags a chain like a guilty thing. She is a woman who wears a mask, like a thing that is a leper. The fire cannot purify her. The waters cannot quench her anguish. Nothing can heal her! No anodyne can give her sleep! No poppies forgetfulness! She is lost! She is a lost soul! That is why I call Lord Illingworth a bad man. That is why I don't want my boy to be with him.

Scenes from Oscar Wilde

A WOMAN OF NO IMPORTANCE ACT 4

(Mrs Arbuthnot responds to her son, Gerald, He has begged his mother to marry Lord Illingworth, his biological father. He feels Lord Illingworth should do the honourable thing by his mother, Mrs Arbuthnot. However, she is not convinced).

<u>Mrs Arbuthnot:</u>
But, Gerald – it is I who refuse. I will not marry Lord Illingworth. I will not marry him.

You talk of atonement for a wrong done. What atonement can be made to me? There is no atonement possible. I am disgraced; he is not. That is all. It is the usual history of a man and a woman as it usually happens, as it always happens. And the ending is the ordinary ending. The woman suffers. The man goes free. I refuse to marry Lord Illingworth.

If he came himself, which he will not do, my answer would be the same. Remember, I am your mother.

I owe nothing to other women. There is not one of them to help me. There is not one woman in the world to whom I could go for pity, if I would take it, or for sympathy, if I could win it. Women are hard on each other. That girl, last night, good though she is, fled from the room as though I were a tainted thing. She was right. I am a tainted thing. But my wrongs are my own, and I will bear them alone. I must bear them alone. What have women who have not sinned to do with me, or I with them? We do not understand each other. What son has ever asked of his mother to make so hideous a sacrifice? None.

I will never stand before God's altar and ask God's blessing on so hideous a mockery as a marriage between me and George Harford. I will not say the words the Church bids us to say. I will not say them. I dare not. How could I swear to love the man I loathe, to honour him who wrought you dishonor, to obey him who, in his mastery, made me to sin? No, marriage is a sacrament for those who love each other. It is not for such as him, or such as me. Gerald, to save you from the world's sneers and taunts I have lied to the world. For twenty years I have lied to the world. I could not tell the world the truth. Who can ever? But not for my own sake will I lie to God, and in God's presence. No, Gerald, no ceremony, shall ever bind me to George Harford. It may be that I am too bound to him already, who, robbing me, yet left me richer, so that in the mire of my life I found the pearl of price, or what I thought would be so.

A WOMAN OF NO IMPORTANCE ACT 4

(Mrs Arbuthnot is talking to her son, Gerald, on the subject of motherhood).

<u>Mrs Arbuthnot:</u>
Men don't understand what mothers are. I am no different from other women except in the wrong done me and the wrong I did, and my very heavy punishments and great disgrace. And yet, to bear you, I had to look on death. To nurture you, I had to wrestle with it. Death fought with me for you. All women have to fight with death to keep their children. Death, being childless, wants our children from us. Gerald, when you were naked, I clothed you, when you were hungry, I gave you food. Night and day all that long winter I tended you. No office is too mean, no care too lowly for the thing we women love – and oh! How I loved you. Not Hannah, Samuel more. And you needed love, for you were weakly, and only love could have kept you alive. Only love can keep anyone alive. And boys are careless often and without thinking give pain, and we always fancy that when they come to a man's estate and know us better, they will repay us. But it is not so. The world draws them from our side, and they make friends with whom they are happier than they are with us, and have amusements from which we are barred, and interests that are not ours; and they are unjust to us often, for when they find life bitter they blame us for it, and when they find it sweet we do not taste its' sweetness with them ... You made many friends and went into their houses and were glad with them, and I, knowing my secret, did not dare to follow, but stayed home and closed the door, shut out the sun and sat in the darkness. What should I have done in honest households? My past was ever with me ...And you thought I didn't care for the pleasant things in life. I tell you I longed for them, but did not dare to touch them, feeling I had no right. You thought I was happier working amongst the poor. That was my mission, you imagined. It was not, but where else was I to go? The sick do not ask if the hand that smooths their pillow is pure, nor the dying care if the lips that touch their brow have known the kiss of sin. It was you I thought of all the time; I gave to them the love you did not need: Lavished on them a love that was not theirs ... And you thought I spend too much of my time going to Church,

and in Church duties. But where else could I turn? God's house is the only house where sinners are made welcome, and you were always in my heart, Gerald, too much in my heart. For, though day after day, at morn or evensong, I have knelt in God's house, I have never repented to my sin. How could I repent of my sin when you, my love, were its' fruit? Even now that you are bitter to me, I cannot repent. I do not. You are more to me than innocence. I would rather by your mother – oh! much rather! – than have been always pure … Oh, don't you see? Don't you understand? It is my dishonor that has made you so dear to me. It is my disgrace that has bound you so closely to me. It is the price I paid for you – that makes me love you as I do. Oh, don't ask me to do this horrible thing. Child of my shame, be still the child of my shame!

LADY WINDERMERE'S FAN 1892

Act One begins with birthday preparations for Lady Windermere. Lord Darlington visits her at home to wish her felicitations. Lady Windermere reprimands him for flirting with her and he responds by suggesting that her husband is being unfaithful to her. The Duchess of Berwick also pays her a visit and mentions that Lord Windermere has been spending rather too much time with a Mrs Erlynne, of a questionable status. On learning this, Lady Windermere searches her husband's papers and discovers that payments have been made to Mrs Erlynne. To exascerbate things further,Lord Windermere intends to invite Mrs Erlynne to the birthday celebration that evening and Lady Windermere is outraged and refuses to receive her. However, Lord Windermere ignore his wife's refusal and invites her anyway. Lord Windermere, in a moment alone, expresses concern that his wife may find out Mrs Erlynne's identity.

In Act Two, the party begins. Mrs Erlynne is particularly flirtatious with the male guests. Lady Windermere, still mad with her husband, allows Lord Darlington to flirt with her. Darlington expresses his love for her and begs Lady Windermere to leave England with him. Lady Windermere writes a letter to her husband explaining that she is leaving him but Mrs Erlynne discovers the letter.

In Act Three, Mrs Erlynne visits Lady Windermere in Lord Darlington's rooms and explains she has not been having an affair, neither is she in love with Lord Windemere. Therefore, she should not make the dreadful mistake of leaving her husband. Lord Darlington, Lord Augustus and Lord Windermere return to Darlington's rooms and the two women are forced to hide themselves. Lord Windermere finds his wife's fan in the apartment and suspects his wife of being there. Mrs Erlynne quickly emerges from her hiding place, claiming it was she who took Lady Windermere's fan, by mistake.

In Act Four, Lady Windermere has a change of heart regarding Mrs Erlynne, much to her husband's astonishment. Her husband wishes to take a trip to the countryside and Lady Windermere insists she visits Mrs Erlynne before they leave. Mrs Erlynne requests a photograph of Lady Windermere with her child, and on leaving the room in order to grant this request, Mrs Erlynne speaks in private to Lord Windermere. She reveals that she is his wife's long-lost mother. She manages to persuade Lady Windermere, her daughter, not to leave her husband as she is convinced that he loves her deeply. The play ends happily with the couple reconciling their differences and Lord Augustus proposing to Mrs Erlynne.

LADY WINDERMERE'S FAN ACT 1

(The Duchess of Berwick is talking to Lady Windermere about Lord Windermere's strange behavior towards Mrs Erlynne).

Duchess of Berwick:
Only last night at dear Lady Jansen's, everyone was saying how extraordinary it was that, of all men in London, Windermere should behave in such a way.

He goes to see her continually, and stops for hours at a time, and while he is there, she is not at home to anyone. Not that many ladies call on her, dear, but she has a great many disreputable men friends – my own brother particularly, as I told you – and that is what makes it so dreadful about Windermere. We looked upon *him* as being such a model husband, but I am afraid there is no doubt about it. My dear nieces – you know the Saville girls, don't you? – such nice domestic creatures – plain, dreadfully plain, - but so good – well, they're always at the window doing fancy work, and making ugly things for the poor, which I think so useful of them in these dreadful socialistic days, and this terrible woman has taken a house in Curzon Street, right opposite them – such a respectable street, too! I don't know what we're coming to! And they tell me that Windermere goes there four or five times a week – they *see* him. They can't help it – and although they never talk scandal, they – well, of course – they remark on it to everyone. And the worst of it all is that I have been told that this woman has got a great deal of money out of somebody, for it seems that she came to London six months ago without anything at all to speak of, and now she has this charming house in Mayfair, drives her ponies in the Park every afternoon and all – well, all – since she has known poor dear Windermere.

But it's quite true, my dear. The whole of London knows it. That is why I felt it was better to come and talk to you, and advise you to take Windermere away at once to Hamburg or to Aix, where he'll have something to amuse him, and where you can watch him all day long. I assure you, my dear, that on several occasions after I was first married, I had to pretend to be very ill, and was obliged to drink the most unpleasant mineral waters, merely to get Berwick out of town. He was so extremely susceptible. Though I am bound to say he never gave away any large sums of money to anybody. He is far too high-principled for that!

Don't take this little aberration of Windermere's too much to heart. Just take him abroad, and he'll come back to you all right.

LADY WINDERMERE'S FAN ACT 2

(Mrs Erlynne is talking to Lord Windemere. She informs him that Augustus has proposed to her and that she intends to accept him. She asks Windermere to finance her).

Mrs Erlynne:
Charming ball it has been! Quite reminds me of old days. (*She sits on a sofa*). And I see that there are just as many fools in society as there used to be. So pleased to find that nothing has altered! Except Margaret. She's grown quite pretty. The last time I saw her – twenty years ago, she was a fright in flannel. Positive fright, I assure you! The dear Duchess! And that sweet Lady Agatha! Just the type of girl I like! Well, really, Windermere, if I am to be the Duchess's sister in law –

Oh, yes! He's to call tomorrow at twelve o'clock. He wanted to propose tonight. In fact, he did. He kept on proposing. Poor Augustus; you know how he repeats himself. Such a bad habit. But I told him I wouldn't give him an answer till tomorrow. Of course, I am going to take him. And I dare say I'll make him an admirable wife, as wives go. And there is a great deal of good in Lord Augustus. Fortunately, it is all on the surface. Just where good qualities should be. Of course, you must help me in this matter.

Oh, no! I do the encouraging. But you will make me a handsome settlement, Windermere, won't you?

We will talk of it on the terrace. Even business should have a picturesque background. Should it now, Windermere? With a proper background, women can do anything.

Tomorrow I am going to accept him. And I think it would be a good thing if I was able to tell him that I had – well, what shall I say? - £2000 a year left to me by a third cousin – or a second husband – or some distant relative of that kind. It would be an additional attraction, wouldn't it? You have a delightful opportunity now of paying me a compliment, Windermere. But you are not very clever at paying compliments. I am afraid Margaret doesn't encourage you in that excellent habit. It's a great mistake on her part. When men give up saying what is charming, they give up thinking what is charming. But seriously, what do you say to £2000? £2500, I think. In modern life margin is everything. Windermere, don't you think the world an intensely amusing place? I do!

LADY WINDERMERE'S FAN ACT 3

(Mrs Erlynne urges Lady Windermere to return to her husband, Lord Windermere. She assures her that her husband loves her deeply. She also stresses the importance of maintaining her marriage for the sake of their child).

Mrs Erlynne:
Believe what you choose about me. I am not worth a moment's sorrow. But don't spoil your beautiful young life on my account! You don't know what may be in store for you, unless you leave this house at once. You don't know what it is to fall into the pit, to be despised, mocked, abandoned, sneered at – to be an outcast! To find the door shut against one, to have to creep in by hideous byways, afraid every moment lest the mask should be stripped from one's face, and all the while to hear the laughter, the horrible laughter of the world, a thing more tragic than all the tears the world has ever shed. You don't know what it is. One pays for one's sin, and then one pays again, and all one's life one pays. You must never know that. As for me, if suffering be an expiation, then at this moment I have expiated all my faults, whatever they have been; for tonight you have made a heart in one who had it not, made it and broken it. – But let it pass. I may have wrecked my own life, but I will not let you wreck yours. You – why you are a mere girl, you would be lost. You couldn't stand dishonor! No! Go back, Lady Windermere, to the husband who loves you, whom you love. You have a child, Lady Windermere. Go back to that child, who even now, in pain or in joy, may be calling to you. God gave you that child. He will require from you that you make his life fine, that you watch over him. What answer will you make to God if his life is ruined through you? Back to your house, Lady Windermere – your husband loves you! He has never swerved for a moment from the love he bears you. But even if he had a thousand loves, you must stay with your child. If he was harsh to you, you must stay with your child. If he ill-treated you, you must stay with your child. If he abandoned you, your place is with your child.

Scenes from Oscar Wilde

LADY WINDERMERE'S FAN ACT 3

(Lady Windermere is at her wits end. She is waiting at Lord Darlington's room. She has left a letter for her husband and is now regretting her decision and is hoping her husband will come and take her back).

<u>Lady Windermere:</u>
Why doesn't he come? This waiting is horrible. He should be here. Why is he not here, to wake by passionate words some fire within me? I am cold – cold as a loveless thing. Arthur must have read my letter by this time. If he cared for me, he would have come after me, would have taken me back by force. But he doesn't care. He's entrammeled by this woman – fascinated by her – dominated by her. If a woman wants to hold a man, she merely has to appeal to what is worst in him. We make gods of men and they leave us. Others make brutes of them and they fawn and are faithful. How hideous life is! … Oh! It was made of me to come here, horribly mad. And yet, which is the worst, I wonder, to be at the mercy of a man who loves one, or the wife of a man who in one's own house dishonours one? What woman knows? What woman in the whole world? But will he love me always, this man to whom I am giving my life? What do I bring to him? Lips that have lost the note of joy, eyes that are blinded by tears, chill hands and icy heart. I bring him nothing. I must go back – no; I can't go back! My letter has put me in their power – Arthur would not take me back! That fatal letter! No! Lord Darlington leaves England tomorrow. I will go with him – I have no choice.

(She sits down for a moment. Then stands to put on her cloak)

No, No! I will go back, let Arthur do with me what he pleases. I can't wait here. It has been madness my coming. I must go at once. As for Lord Darlington – Oh! here he is! What shall I do? What can I say to him? Will he let me go away at all? I have heard that men are brutal, horrible … Oh!

(She buries her face in her hands).

LADY WINDERMERE'S FAN ACT 4

(Lady Windermere is contemplating how to tell her husband, the fact that she has changed her opinion of Mrs Erlynne).

Lady Windermere:
How can I tell him? I can't tell him. It would kill me. I wonder what happened after I escaped from that horrible room. Perhaps she told them the true reason of her being there, and the real meaning of that – fatal fan of mine. Oh, if he knows – how can I look him in the face again? He would never forgive me. How securely one thinks one lives – out of reach of temptation, sin, folly. And then suddenly

– Oh! Life is terrible. It rules us, we do not rule it.

(She rings for the maid)

Have you found out at what time Lord Windermere came in last night?

Five o'clock? He knocked at my door this morning, didn't he? It doesn't matter. Tell Parker not to trouble. That will do.

(Lady Windermere is alone again)

She is sure to tell him. I can fancy a person doing a wonderful act of self-sacrifice, doing it spontaneously, recklessly, nobly – and afterwards fining out that it costs too much. Why should she hesitate between her ruin and mine? ... How strange! I would have publicly disgraced her in my own house. She accepts public disgrace in the house of another to save me ... There is bitter irony in things, a bitter irony in the way we talk of good and bad women... Oh, what a lesson! And what a pity that in life we only get out lessons when they are of no use to us! For even if she doesn't tell, I must. Oh! The shame of it, the shame of it. To tell it is to live through it all again. Actions are the first tragedy in life, words are the second. Words are perhaps the worst. Words are merciless .... Oh!

(Lord Windermere enters)

Yes, I am crying, for I have something to tell you, Arthur. Let us go away today. No, I can't go away today, Arthur. There is someone I must see before I leave town – someone who has been kind to me.

Arthur, Arthur, don't talk so bitterly about any woman. I don't think now that people can be divided into the good and the bad as though they were two separate races or creations. What are called good women may have terrible things in them, mad moods of recklessness, assertion, jealousy, sin. Bad women, as they are termed, may have in them sorrow, repentance, pity, sacrifice. And I don't think Mrs Erlynne a bad woman – I know she's not.
She came here once as *your* guest. She must come now as *mine*. That is but fair.

Scenes from Oscar Wilde

LADY WINDERMERE'S FAN ACT 4

(Mrs Erlynne is planning on leaving and has come to say goodbye. She is talking to Lord Windermere).

Mrs Erlynne:
I have come to bid good-bye to my dear daughter, of course. Oh, don't imagine I am going to have a pathetic scene with her, weep on her neck and tell her who I am, and all that kind of thing. I have no ambition to play the part of a mother. Only once in my life have I known a mother's feelings. That was last night. They were terrible – they made me suffer – they made me suffer too much. For twenty years, as you say, I have lived childless – I want to live childless still. Besides, my dear Windermere, how on earth could I pose as a mother with a grown-up daughter? Margaret is twenty-one, and I have never admitted that I am more than twenty-nine, or thirty at the most. Twenty-nine when there are pink shades, thirty when there are not. So, you see what difficulties it would involve. No, as far as I am concerned, let your wife cherish the memory of this dead, stainless mother. Why should I interfere with her illusions? I find it hard enough to keep my own. I lost one illusion last night. I thought I had no heart. I find I have, and heart doesn't suit me, Windermere. Somehow it doesn't go with modern dress. It makes one look old. And it spoils one's career at critical moments.

I suppose, Windermere, you would like me to retire into a convent, or become a hospital nurse, or something of that kind, as people do in silly modern novels. That is stupid of you, Arthur; in real life we don't do such things – not as long as we have any good looks left, at any rate. No- what consoles one nowadays is not repentance, but pleasure. Repentance is quite out of date. And besides, if a woman really repents, she has to go to a bad dress-maker, otherwise no one believes in her. And nothing in the world would induce me to do that. No; I am going to pass entirely out of your two lives. My coming into them has been a mistake – I discovered that last night.

I regret my bad actions. You regret your good ones - that is the difference between us.

If you tell her, I will make my name so infamous that it will mar every moment of her life. It will ruin her, and make her wretched. If you dare to tell her, there is no depth of degradation I will not sink to, no pit of shame I will not enter. You shall not tell her – I forbid you.

If I said to you that I cared for her, perhaps loved her even – you would sneer at me, wouldn't you?

Don't let us talk any more about it – as for telling my daughter who I am, that I do not allow. It is my secret, it is not yours. If I make up my mind to tell her, and I think I will, I shall tell her before I leave the house – if not, I shall never tell her.

Scenes from Oscar Wilde

SALOME (1891)

(This play originates from the biblical story, Salome. Salome is the stepdaughter of Herod Antipas. Her mother is Herodias. Salome lusts after Jokanaan and is famous for demanding his head on a silver platter. Salome dances the dance of the seven veils before the platter arrives with the head of Jokanaan. Jokanaan is otherwise known as John the Baptist).

Salome:
Thy body is hideous. It is likely the body of a leper. It is like a plastered wall, where vipers have crawled; like a plastered wall where the scorpions have made their nest. It is like a whited sepulchre, full of loathsome things. It is horrible, thy body is horrible. It is of thy hair that I am enamoured, Jokanaan. Thy hair is like clusters of grapes, like the clusters of black grapes that hang from the vine-trees of Edom in the land of the Edomites. Thy hair Is like the cedars of Lebanon, like the great cedars of Lebanon that give their shade to the lions and the robbers who would hide them by day. The long black nights, when the moon hides her face, when the stars are afraid, are not so black as thy hair … Suffer me to touch thy hair.
(She touches his hair)
Thy hair is horrible. It is covered with mire and dust. It is like a crown of thorns placed on thy head. It is like a knot of serpents coiled round thy neck. I love not thy hair … it is thy mouth that I desire, Jokanaan. Thy mouth is like a band of scarlet on a tower of ivory. The pomegranate flowers that blossom in the gardens of Tyre, and are redder than roses, are not so red. The red blasts of trumpets that herald the approach of kings, and make afraid the enemy, are not so red. Thy mouth is redder than the feet of those who tread the wine in the wine-press. It is redder than the feet of the doves who inhabit the temples and are fed by the priests. It is redder than the feet of him who cometh from a forest where he hath slain a lion, and seen gilded tigers. Thy mouth is like a branch of coral that they keep for the kings! It is like the vermilion that the kings take from them. It is like the bow of the King of the Persians, that is painted with vermilion, and is tipped with coral. There is nothing in the world so red as thy mouth … Suffer me to kiss thy mouth.

Scenes from Oscar Wilde

VERA, or The Nihilists Act 1(1883)

(This play is a melodramatic tragedy set in Russia. It tells the story of Vera Sabouroff, a young peasant woman who wishes to overthrow the Czar and his government).

Vera:
God save the people!

The man Ivan whom men called the Czar strikes now at our mother with a dagger deadlier than any ever forged by tyranny against a people's life!

Tomorrow martial law is to be proclaimed over all Russia.

The last right to which the people clung has been taken from them. Without trial, without appeal, without accuser even, our brothers will be taken from their houses, shot in the streets like dogs, sent away to die in the snow, to starve in the dungeon, to rot in the mine. Do you know what martial law means? It means the strangling of a whole nation. The streets will be filled with soldiers' night and day; there will be sentinels at every door. No man dare walk abroad now but the spy or the traitor. Cooped up in the dens we hide in, meeting by stealth, speaking with bated breath; what good can we do now for Russia?

The hour is now come to annihilate and to revenge. Now, we, the Nihilists, have given the people the tree of knowledge to eat of, and the day of silent suffering is over for Russia.
It is the signal for revolution.

Here is the proclamation. I stole it myself at the ball tonight from a young fool, one of Prince Paul's secretaries, who had been given it to copy. It was that which made me so late.

Martial law! O God, how easy it is for a king to kill his people by thousands, but we cannot rid ourselves of one crowned man in Europe! What is there of awful majesty in these men which makes the hand unsteady, the dagger treacherous, the pistol-shot harmless? Are they not men of like passions with ourselves, vulnerable to the same diseases, of flesh and blood not different from our own? What made Olgiati tremble at the supreme crisis of that Roman life, and Guido's nerve fail him when he should have been of iron and steel? A plague, I say, on these fools of Naples, Berlin, and Spain! Methinks that if I stood face to face with one of the crowned men my eye would see more clearly, my aim to be more sure, my whole body gain a strength and power that was not my own! Oh, to think what stands between us and freedom in Europe! A few old men, wrinkled, feeble, tottering dotards whom a boy could strangle for a ducat, or a woman stab in a night-time. These are the things that keep us from liberty. But now methinks the blood of men is dead and the dull earth grown sick of childbearing, else would no crowned dog pollute God's air by living.

THE DECAY OF LYING (An Observation) (1891)

(This play is a duologue between two characters, Cyril and Vivian. Cyril and Vivian are the names of Oscar Wilde's own two sons. Vivian is actually a young man but this scene could easily be played by a female actor. Cyril and Vivian are in the library of a county house in Nottinghamshire. Vivian is writing an article called "The Decay of Lying': A Protest". She is writing is for the 'Retrospective Review. This is an example of Wilde's aesthetic writing).

<u>Vivian:</u>
Enjoy nature! I am glad to say that I have entirely lost that faculty. People tell us that Art makes us love Nature more than we loved her before; that it reveals her secrets to us; and that after a careful study of Corot and Constable we see things in her that had escaped our observation. My own experience is that the more we study Art, the less we care for Nature. What Art really reveals to us is Nature's lack of design, her curious crudities, her extraordinary monotony, her absolutely unfinished condition. Nature has good intentions, of course, but, as Aristotle once said, she cannot carry them out. When I look at a landscape, I cannot help seeing all its defects. It is fortunate for us, however, that Nature is so imperfect, as otherwise we should have no art at all. Art is our spirited protest, our gallant attempt to teach nature her proper place. As for the infinite variety of Nature, that is a pure myth. It is not be found in Nature herself. It resides in the imagination, or fancy, or cultivated blindness of the man who looks at her.

Nature is so uncomfortable. Grass is hard and lumpy and damp, and full of dreadful black insects. Why, even Morris's poorest workman could make you a more comfortable seat than the whole of Nature can. Nature pales before the furniture of "the street which from Oxford has borrowed its name," as the poet you love so much once vilely phrased it. I don't complain. If nature had been comfortable, mankind would never have invented architecture, and I prefer houses to the open air. In a house we all feel of the proper proportions. Everything is subordinated to us, fashioned for our use and our pleasure. Egotism itself, which is so necessary to a proper sense of human dignity, is entirely the result of indoor life. Out of doors one becomes abstract and impersonal. One's individuality absolutely leaves one. And then Nature's so indifferent, so unappreciative. Whenever I am walking in the park here, I always feel that I am no more to her than the cattle that browse on the slope, or the burdock that blooms in the ditch. Nothing is more evident than that Nature hates Mind. Thinking is the most unhealthy thing in the world, and people die of it just as they die of any other disease. Fortunately, in England at any rate, thought is not catching. Our splendid physique as a people is entirely due to our national stupidity. I only hope we shall be able to keep this great historic bulwark of our happiness for many years to come; but I am afraid that we are beginning to be over-educated; at least everybody who is incapable of learning has taken to teaching – that is really what our enthusiasm for education has come to. In the meantime, you had better go back to your wearisome uncomfortable Nature, and leave me to correct my proofs.

THE DUOLOGUES

Scenes from Oscar Wilde

(Cecily Cardew and Miss Prism, her tutor, are in the garden at the Manor House. It is July. Basket chairs and a table covered with books are set under a large yew tree. Cecily is watering flowers).

Miss Prism:
Cecily, Cecily! Surely such a utilitarian occupation as the watering of flowers is rather Moulton's duty than yours? Especially at a moment when a moment when intellectual pleasures await you. Your German grammar is on the table. Pray open it at page fifteen. We will repeat yesterday's lesson.

Cecily:
But I don't like German. It isn't at all a becoming language. I know perfectly well that I look quite plain after my German lesson.

Miss Prism:
Child, you know how anxious your guardian is that you should improve yourself in every way. He laid particular stress on your German, as he was leaving for town yesterday. Indeed, he always lays stress on your German when he is leaving for town.

Cecily:
Dear Uncle Jack is so very serious! Sometimes he is so serious that I think he cannot be quite well.

Miss Prism:
Your guardian enjoys the best of health, and his gravity of demeanour is especially to be commended in one so comparatively young as his is. I know no one who has a higher sense of duty and responsibility.

Cecily:
I suppose that is why he often looks a little bored when we three are together.

Miss Prism:
Cecily! I am surprised at you. Mr Worthing has many troubles in his life. Idle merriment and triviality would be out of place in his

unfortunate young man, his brother.

Cecily:
I wish Uncle Jack would allow that unfortunate young man, his brother, to come down here sometimes. We might have a good influence over him, Miss Prism. I am sure you certainly would. You know German, and geology, and things of that kind influence a man very much. *(Cecily begins to write in her diary).*

Miss Prism:
I do not think that even I could produce any effect on a character that according to his own brother's admission is irretrievably weak and vacillating. Indeed, I am not sure that I would desire to reclaim him. I am not in favour of this modern mania for turning bad people into good people at a moment's notice. As a man sows so let him reap. You must put away your diary, Cecily. I really don't see why you should keep a diary at all.

Cecily:
I keep a diary in order to enter the wonderful secrets of my life. If I didn't write them down, I should probably forget all about them.

Miss Prism:
Memory, my dear Cecily, is the diary that we all carry about with us.

Cecily:
Yes, but it usually chronicles the things that have never happened, and couldn't possibly have happened. I believe that Memory is responsible for nearly all the three-volume novels that Mudie sends us.

Miss Prism:
Do not speak slightingly of the three-volume novel, Cecily. I wrote one myself in earlier days.

Cecily:
Did you really, Miss Prism? How wonderfully clever you are! I hope it did not end happily? I don't like novels that end happily.

Miss Prism:
The good ended happily, and the bad unhappily. That is what Fiction means.

Cecily:
I suppose so. But it seems very unfair. And was your novel ever published?

Miss Prism:
Alas! No. The manuscript unfortunately was abandoned. I used the word in the sense of lost or mislaid. To your work, child, these speculations are profitless.

(Cecily Cardew is visited by Gwendolen Fairfax in the garden of Jack's country estate).

Cecily:
Pray let me introduce myself to you. My Name is Cecily Cardew.

Gwendolen:
Cecily Cardew? What a very sweet name! Something tells me that we are going to be great friends. I like you already more than I can say. My first impressions of people are never wrong.

Cecily:
How nice of you to like me so much after we have known each other such a comparatively short time. Pray sit down.

Gwendolen: *(still standing up)*
I may call you Cecily, may I not?

Cecily:
With pleasure!

Gwendolen:
And you will always call me Gwendolen, won't you?

Cecily:
If you wish.

Gwendolen:
Then that is all quite settled, is it not?

Cecily:
I hope so. (*They both sit down together*)

Gwendolen:
Perhaps this might be a favourable opportunity for my mentioning who I am. My father is Lord Bracknell. You have never heard of Papa, I suppose?

I don't think so.

Gwendolen:
Outside the family circle, papa, I am glad to say, is entirely unknown. I think that is quite as it should be. The home seems to me to be the proper sphere for the man. And certainly, once a man begins to neglect his domestic duties he becomes painfully effeminate, does he not? And I don't like that. It makes men so very attractive. Cecily, mamma, whose views on education are remarkably strict, has brought me up to be extremely short-sighted; it is part of her system; so do you mind my looking at you through my glasses?

Cecily:
Oh! not at all, Gwendolen. I am very fond of being looked at.

Gwendolen: (*She examines Cecily through a lorgnette*)
You are here on a short visit, I suppose.

Cecily:
Oh no! I live here.

Gwendolen:
Really? Your mother, no doubt, or some female relative of advanced years, resides here also?

Cecily:
Oh no! I have no mother, nor, in fact, any relations.

Gwendolen:
Indeed?

Cecily:
My dear guardian, with the assistance of Miss Prism, has the arduous task of looking after me.

Gwendolen:
Your guardian?

Yes, I am Mr Worthing's ward.

Gwendolen:
Oh! It is strange he never mentioned to me that he had a ward. How secretive of him! He grows more interesting hourly. I am not sure, however, that the news inspires me with feelings of unmixed delight. I am very fond of you, Cecily; I have liked you ever since I met you! But I am bound to state that now that I know that you are Mr Worthing's ward, I cannot help expressing a wish you were – well, just a little older than you seem to be – and not quite so very alluring in appearance. In fact, if I may speak candidly –

Cecily:
Pray do! I think that whenever one has anything unpleasant to say, one should always be quite candid.

Gwendolen:
Well, to speak with perfect candour, Cecily, I wish you were fully forty-two, and more than usually plain for your age. Ernest has a strong upright nature. He is the very soul of truth and honour. Disloyalty would be as impossible to him as deception. But even men of the noblest possible moral character are extremely susceptible to the influence of the physical charms of others. Modern, no less that Ancient History, supplies us with many most painful examples of what I refer to. If it were not so, indeed, History would be quite unreadable.

Cecily:
I beg your pardon, Gwendolen, did you say Ernest?

Gwendolen:
Yes.

Cecily:
Oh, but it is not Mr Ernest Worthing who is my guardian. It is his brother – his elder brother.

Gwendolen:
Ernest never mentioned to me that he had a brother.

Cecily:
I am sorry to say they have not been on good terms for a long time.

Gwendolen:
Ah! That accounts for it. And now that I think of it, I have never heard any man mention his brother. The subject seems distasteful to more men. Cecily, you have lifted a load from my mind. I was growing almost anxious. It would have been terrible if any cloud had come across a friendship like ours, would it not? Of course, you are quite, quite sure that it is not Mr Ernest Worthing who is your guardian?

Cecily:
Quite sure. (*Pause*) In fact, I am going to be his.

Gwendolen:
I beg your pardon?

Cecily: (*confidingly*)
Dearest Gwendolen, there is no reason why I should make a secret of it to you. Our little county newspaper is sure to chronicle the fact next week. Mr Ernest Worthing and I are engaged to be married.

Gwendolen: (*rising*)
My darling Cecily, I think there must be some slight error. Mr Ernest Worthing is engaged to me. The announcement will appear in the *Morning Post* on Saturday at the latest.

Cecily: (*rising*)
I am afraid you must be under some misconception. Ernest proposed to me exactly ten minutes ago. (*She shows her diary*)

Gwendolen:
It is very curious, for he asked me to be his wife yesterday afternoon at 5.30. If you would care to verify the incident, pray do so. (*She produces her own diary*). I never travel without my diary. One should always have something sensation to read in the train.

am afraid I have the prior claim.

Cecily:
It would distress me more that I can tell you, dear Gwendolen, if it has caused you any mental or physical anguish, but I feel bound to point out that since Ernest proposed to you. he clearly has changed his
mind.

Gwendolen:
If the poor fellow has been entrapped into any foolish promise, I shall consider it my duty to rescue him at once, and with a firm hand.

Cecily:
Whatever unfortunate entanglement my dear boy may have got into, I will never reproach him with it after we are married.

Gwendolen:
Do you allude to me, Miss Cardew, as an entanglement? You are presumptuous. On an occasion of this kind it becomes more than a moral duty to speak one's mind. It becomes a pleasure.

Cecily:
Do you suggest, Miss Fairfax, that I entrapped Ernest into an engagement? How dare you? This is no time for wearing the shallow mask of manners. When I see a spade, I call it a spade.

Gwendolen:
I am glad to say that I have never seen a spade. It is obvious that our social spheres have been widely different.

(Merriman brings in the tea on a silver salver)

Are there many interesting walks in the vicinity, Miss Cardew?

Cecily:
Oh! Yes! A great many. From the top of one of the hills quite close one can see five counties.

Gwendolen:
Five counties! I don't think I should like that; I hate crowds.

Cecily:
I suppose that is why you live in town?

Gwendolen:
Quite a well-kept garden this is, Miss Cardew.

Cecily:
So glad you like it, Miss Fairfax.

Gwendolen:
I had no idea there were any flowers in the country.

Cecily:
Oh, flowers are as common here, Miss Fairfax, as people are in London.

Gwendolen:
Personally, I cannot understand how anybody manages to exist in the country, if anybody who is anybody does. The country always bores me to death.

Cecily:
Ah! This is what the newspapers call agricultural depression, is it not? I believe the aristocracy are suffering very much from it just at present. It is almost an epidemic amongst them, I have been told. May I offer you some tea, Miss Fairfax?

Gwendolen:
Thank you. (*Aside*). Detestable girl! But I require tea!

Cecily:
Sugar?

Gwendolen:
No, thank you. Sugar is not fashionable any more.

(Cecily takes the tongs and puts four lumps of sugar into the cup).

Cecily:
Cake or bread and butter?

Gwendolen:
Bread and butter, please. Cake is rarely seen at the best houses nowadays.
(she tastes the tea).
You have filled my tea with lumps of sugar, and though I asked most distinctly for bread and butter, you have given me cake. I am known for the gentleness of my disposition, and the extraordinary sweetness of my nature, but I warn you, Miss Cardew, you may go too far.

Cecily:
To save my poor, innocent, trusting boy from the machinations of any other girl there are no lengths to which I would not go.

Gwendolen:
From the moment I saw you I distrusted you. I felt that you were false and deceitful. I am never deceived in such matters. My first impressions of people are invariably right.

Cecily:
It seems to me, Miss Fairfax, that I am trespassing on your valuable time. No doubt you have many other calls of a similar character to make in the neighbourhood.

(Mrs Cheveley is visiting Gertrude Chiltern's home. Lady Markby has just left and the two women have a moment alone. There is no love lost between the two women. Sir Robert Chiltern enters towards the end of the scene).

Mrs Cheveley:
Wonderful woman, Lady Markby, isn't she? Talks more and says less than anybody I ever met. She is made to be a public speaker. Much more so than her husband, though he is a typical Englishman, always dull and usually violent.

Lady Chiltern:
Mrs Cheveley, I think it is right to tell you quite frankly that, had I known who you really were, I should not have invited you to my house last night.

Mrs Cheveley: *(with an impertinent smile)*
Really?

Lady Chiltern:
I could not have done so.

Mrs Cheveley:
I see that after all these years you have not changed a bit, Gertrude.

Lady Chiltern:
I never change.

Mrs Cheveley:
Then life has taught you nothing?

Lady Chiltern:
It has taught me that a person who has once been guilty of a dishonest and dishonourable action may be guilty of it a second time, and should be shunned.

Would you apply that rule to everyone?

Lady Chiltern:
Yes, to everyone, without exception.

Mrs Cheveley:
Then I am sorry for you, Gertrude, very sorry for you.

Lady Chiltern:
You see now, I am sure, that for many reasons any further acquaintance between us during your stay in London is quite impossible?

Mrs Cheveley:
Do you know, Gertrude, I don't mind your talking morality a bit. Morality is simply the attitude we adopt towards people who we personally dislike. You dislike me. I am quite aware of that. And I have always detested you. And yet I have come here to do you a service.

Lady Chiltern:
Like the service you wished to render my husband last night, I suppose. Thank heaven, I saved him from that.

Mrs Cheveley:
It was you made him write that insolent letter to me? It was you who made him break his promise?

Lady Chiltern:
Yes.

Mrs Cheveley:
Then you must make him keep it. I give you till tomorrow morning – no more. If by the time your husband does not solemnly bind himself to help me in this great scheme in which I am interested –

Lady Chiltern:
This fraudulent speculation –

Mrs Cheveley:
Call it what you choose. I hold your husband in the hollow of my hand, and if you are wise you will make him do what I tell him.

Lady Chiltern:
You are impertinent. What has my husband to do with you? With a woman like you?

Mrs Cheveley:
In this world like meets with like. It is because your husband is himself fraudulent and dishonest that we pair so well together. Between you and him there are chasms. He and I are closer than friends. We are enemies linked together. The same sin binds us.

Lady Chiltern:
How dare you class my husband with yourself? How dare you threaten him or me? Leave my house. You are unfit to enter it.

(Lord Chiltern enters)

Mrs Cheveley:
Your house! A house bought with the price of dishonour. A house, everything in which has been paid for by fraud. Ask him what the origin of his fortune is! Get him to tell you how he sold to a stockbroker a Cabinet secret. Learn from him to what you owe your position.

Lady Chiltern:
It is not true! Robert! It is not true!

Mrs Cheveley:
Look at him! Can he deny it? Does he dare to?
I have not yet finished with you, with either of you. I give you both till tomorrow at noon. If by then you don't do what I bid you to do, the whole world shall know the origin of Robert Chiltern.

LADY WINDERMERE'S FAN ACT 1

(*The Duchess of Berwick addresses Lady Windermere*).

Duchess of Berwick:
And now I must tell you how sorry I am for you, dear Margaret. (*she crosses and sits next to her*)

Lady Windermere:
Why, Duchess?

Duchess of Berwick:
Oh, on account of that horrid woman. She dresses so well, too, which makes it much worse, sets such a dreadful example. Augustus – you know my disreputable brother – such a trial to us all – well, Augustus is completely infatuated about her. It is quite scandalous, for she is absolutely inadmissible into society. Many a woman has a past, but I am told that she has at least a dozen, and they all fit.

Lady Windermere:
Whom are you talking about, Duchess?

Duchess of Berwick:
About Mrs Erlynne?

Lady Windermere:
I never heard of her, Duchess. And what has she to do with me?

Duchess of Berwick:
My poor child!

Lady Windermere:
Why do you talk to me about this person?

Duchess of Berwick:
Don't you really know? I assure you we're all so distressed about it. Only last night at dear Lady Jansen's everyone was saying how extraordinary it was that, of all men in London, Windermere should

Lady Windermere:
My husband - what has he got to do with any woman of that kind?

Duchess of Berwick:
Ah, what indeed, dear? That is the point. He goes to see her continually, and stops for hours at a time, and while he is there, she is not at home to anyone. Not that many ladies call on her, dear, but she has a great many disreputable men friends – my own brother particularly, as I told you – and that is what makes it so dreadful about Windermere. We looked upon *him* as being such a model husband, but I am afraid there is no doubt about it. My dear nieces – you know the Saville girls, don't you? – such nice domestic creatures – plain, dreadfully plain, - but so good – well, they're always at the window doing fancy work, and making ugly things for the poor, which I think so useful of them in these dreadful socialistic days, and this terrible woman has taken a house in Curzon Street, right opposite them – such a respectable street, too! I don't know what we're coming to! And they tell me that Windermere goes there four or five times a week – they *see* him. They can't help it – and although they never talk scandal, they – well, of course – they remark on it to everyone. And the worst of it all is that I have been told that this woman has got a great deal of money out of somebody, for it seems that she came to London six months ago without anything at all to speak of, and now she has this charming house in Mayfair, drives her ponies in the Park every afternoon and all – well, all – since she has known poor dear Windermere.

Lady Windermere:
Oh, I can't believe it!

Duchess of Berwick:
But it's quite true, my dear. The whole of London knows it. That is why I felt it was better to come and talk to you, and advise you to take Windermere away at once to Hamburg or to Aix, where he'll have something to amuse him, and where you can watch him all day long. I assure you, my dear, that on several occasions after I was first married, I had to pretend to be very ill, and was obliged to

out of town. He was so extremely susceptible. Though I am bound to say he never gave away any large sums of money to anybody. He is far too high-principled for that!

Lady Windermere:
Duchess, Duchess, it's impossible! We are only married two years. Our child is but six months old.

Duchess of Berwick:
Ah, the dear pretty baby! How is the little darling? Is it a boy or a girl? I hope a girl – ah, no, I remember it's a boy! I'm so sorry. Boys are so wicked. My boy is excessively immoral. You wouldn't believe at what hours he comes home. And he's only left Oxford a few months – I really don't know what they teach them there.

Lady Windermere:
Are all men bad?

Duchess of Berwick:
Oh, all of them, my dear, all of them, without any exception. And they never grow any better. Men become old, but they never become good.

Lady Windermere:
Windermere and I married for love.

Duchess of Berwick:
Yes, we begin like that. It was only Berwick's brutal and incessant threats of suicide that made me accept him at all and before the year was out, he was running after all kinds of petticoats, every colour, every shape, every material. In fact, before the honeymoon was over, I caught him winking at my maid, a most pretty, respectable girl. I dismissed her at once without a character. No, I remember I passed her on to my sister; poor dear Sir George is so short-sighted, I thought it wouldn't matter. But it did, though – it was most unfortunate. And now my dear child, I must go, as we are dining out. And mind you don't take this little aberration of Windermere's too much to heart. Just take him abroad, and he'll come back to you all right.

LADY WINDERMERE'S FAN ACT 3

(In Lord Darlington's rooms. Mrs Erlynne pays a visit to Lady Windermere).

Mrs Erlynne:
Lady Windermere! (*Lady Windermere is startled*). Thank Heaven I am in time. You must go back to your husband's house immediately.

Lady Windermere:
Must?

Mrs Erlynne:
Yes, you must! There is not a second to be lost. Lord Darlington may return at any moment.

Lady Windermere:
Don't come near me!

Mrs Erlynne:
Oh! You are on the brink of ruin, you are on the brink of a hideous precipice. You must leave this place at once; my carriage is waiting at the corner of the street. You must come with me and drive straight home.

(Lady Windermere throws off her cloak & flings it on the sofa)

What are you doing?

Lady Windermere:
Mrs Erlynne – if you had not come here, I would have gone back. But now that I see you, I feel that nothing in the whole world would induce me to live under the same roof as Lord Windermere. You fill me with horror. There is something about you that stirs the wildest- rage within me. And I know why you are here. My husband sent you to lure me back that I might serve as a blind to whatever relations exist between you and him.

Mrs Erlynne:
Oh! You don't think that – you can't.

Lady Windermere:
Go back to my husband, Mrs Erlynne. He belongs to you and not to me. I suppose he is afraid of a scandal. Men are such cowards. They outrage every law of the world, and are afraid of the world's tongue. But he had better prepare himself. He shall have a scandal. He shall have the worst scandal there has been in London for years. He shall see his name in every vile paper, mine on every hideous placard.

Mrs Erlynne:
No – no –

Lady Windermere:
Yes! He shall. Had he come himself, I admit I would have gone back to the life of degradation you and he had prepared for me – I was going back – but to stay himself at home, and to send you as his messenger – oh! It was infamous – infamous.

Mrs Erlynne:
Lady Windermere, you wrong me horribly – you wrong your husband horribly. He doesn't know you are here – he thinks you are safe in your own house. He thinks you are asleep in your own room. He never read the mad letter you wrote to him!

Lady Windermere:
Never read it!

Mrs Erlynne:
No – he knows nothing about it.

Lady Windermere:
How simple you think me! You are lying to me!

Mrs Erlynne:
I am not. I am telling the truth.

Lady Windermere:
If my husband didn't read the letter, how is it that you are here? Who told you I had left the house you were shameless enough to enter: who told you where I had gone? My husband told you, and sent you to decoy me back.

Mrs Erlynne:
Your husband has never seen the letter. I- saw it, I opened it. I- read it.

Lady Windermere:
You opened a letter of mine to my husband? You wouldn't dare!

Mrs Erlynne:
Dare! Oh! To save you from the abyss into which you are falling, there is nothing in the world I would not dare, nothing in the world. Here is the letter. Your husband has never read it. He never shall read it. It should never have been written.

(*She tears it up and throws it into the fire*)

Lady Windermere:
How do I know that that was my letter after all? You seem to think that commonest device can take me in!

Mrs Erlynne:
Oh! Why do you disbelieve everything I tell you? What object do you think I have in coming here, except to save you from utter ruin, to save you from the consequence of a hideous mistake? That letter that is burnt now was *your* letter. I swear it to you!

Lady Windermere:
You took good care to burn it before I had examined it. I cannot trust you. You, whose whole life is a lie, how could you speak the truth about anything?

Mrs Erlynne:
Think as you like about me – say what you choose against me,

Lady Windermere:
I do not love him!

Mrs Erlynne:
You do, and you know that he loves you.

Lady Windermere:
He does not understand what love is. He understands it as little as you do – but I see what you want. It would be a great advantage for you to get me back. Dear Heaven! What a life I would have then! Living at the mercy of a woman who has neither mercy nor pity in her, a woman whom it is an infamy to meet, a degradation to know, a vile woman, a woman who comes between husband and wife!

Mrs Erlynne:
Lady Windermere, Lady Windermere, don't say such terrible things. You don't know how terrible they are, how terrible and how unjust. Listen, you must listen! Only go back to your husband, and I promise you never to communicate with him again on any pretext – never to see him= never to have anything to do with his life or yours. The money that he gave me, he gave me not through love, but through hatred, not in worship, but in contempt. The hold I have over him –

Lady Windermere:
Ah! You admit you have a hold!

Mrs Erlynne:
Yes, and I will tell you what it is. It is his love for you, Lady Windermere.

Lady Windermere:
You expect me to believe that?

Mrs Erlynne:
You must believe it! It is true. It is his love for you that has made him submit to – oh! Call it what you like, tyranny, threats, anything

shame, yes, shame and disgrace.

Lady Windermere:
What do you mean? You are insolent! What have I to do with you?

Mrs Erlynne:
Nothing. I know it – but I tell you that your husband loves you – that you may never meet with such love again in your whole life – and that if you throw it away, the day may come when you will starve for love and it will not be given to you, beg for love and it will be denied you. Oh! Arthur loves you!

Lady Windermere:
Arthur? And you tell me there is nothing between you?

Mrs Erlynne:
Lady Windermere, before Heaven your husband is guiltless of all offence towards you! And I – I tell you that if, had it ever occurred to me, that such a monstrous suspicion would have entered your mind, I would have died rather than have crossed your life or his – died, gladly died!

Lady Windermere:
You talk as if you had a heart. Women like you have no hearts. Heart is not in you. You are bought and sold.

Mrs Erlynne:
Believe what you choose about me. But don't spoil your beautiful young life on my account! You don't know what may be in store for you, unless you leave this house at once. You don't know what it is to find the door shut against one, to have to creep in by hideous byways. You don't know what it is. One pays for one's sin, and then one pays again, and all one's life one pays. You must never know that. I may have wrecked my own life, but I will not let you wreck yours. You have neither the wit, nor the courage. You couldn't stand dishonor! No! Go back, Lady Windermere, to the husband who loves you, whom you love. You have a child, Lady Windermere. Go back to that child, who even now, in pain or in joy, may be calling to you. God gave you that child. He will require

to your house, Lady Windermere – your husband loves you! He has never swerved for a moment from the love he bears you. But even if he had a thousand loves, you must stay with your child. If he was harsh to you, you must stay with your child. If he ill-treated you, you must stay with your child. If he abandoned you, your place is with your child.

(Lady Windermere burst into tears)

Lady Windermere:
Take me home. Take me home.

Mrs Erlynne:
Come! Where is your cloak? Put it on. Come at once.

Lady Windermere:
Stop! Don't you hear voices? Yes, there is! That is my husband's voice! He is coming in! Save me! Oh, it's some plot! You have sent for him.

Mrs Erlynne:
Silence! I'm here to save you, if I can.

ABOUT THE AUTHOR

Kim Gilbert trained as a professional actress at the Guildford School of Acting, Guildhall School of Music and Drama and at the Open University. She has been acting, teaching and directing plays and musical productions for more than 35 years. She has experience in a wide range of theatre, TV and voiceover work. She has a First-class Honours degree in English and has taught English and Drama in many top schools in the country. Kim has examined for Lamda for a number of years and has been running Dramatic Arts Studio for 11 years, a private drama studio which specialises in developing excellence in all forms of performance and communication.

www.dramaticartsstudio.com

Other Books by the same author:

<u>Shakespeare Scenes</u>

Monologues for young female actors
Monologues for young adult female actors
Duologues for female actors
Monologues for young male actors

<u>Chekhov Scenes</u>

Monologues & Duologues for women

Available from Amazon Bookstore

"Thanks for reading! If you enjoyed this book or found it useful, I'd be very grateful if you'd post a short review on Amazon. Your support really does make a difference and I read all the reviews personally so I can get your feedback and make this book even better.

Thanks again for your support!"

ABOUT THE AUTHOR

Kim Gilbert trained as a professional actress at the Guildford School of Acting, Guildhall School of Music and Drama and at the Open University. She has been acting, teaching and directing plays and musical productions for more than 35 years. She has experience in a wide range of theatre, TV and voiceover work. She has a First-class Honours degree in English and has taught English and Drama in many top schools in the country. Kim has examined for Lamda for a number of years and has been running Dramatic Arts Studio for 11 years, a private drama studio which specialises in developing excellence in all forms of performance and communication.

www.dramaticartsstudio.com

Other Books by the same author:

Shakespeare Scenes

Monologues for young female actors
Monologues for young adult female actors
Duologues for female actors
Monologues for young male actors

Chekhov Scenes

Monologues & Duologues for women

Available from Amazon Bookstore

"Thanks for reading! If you enjoyed this book or found it useful, I'd be very grateful if you'd post a short review on Amazon. Your support really does make a difference and I read all the reviews personally so I can get your feedback and make this book even better.

Thanks again for your support!"